Computer Manual in MATLAB
to Accompany
Pattern Classification

Second Edition

David G. Stork
Elad Yom-Tov

WILEY-
INTERSCIENCE

A JOHN WILEY & SONS, INC., PUBLICATION

Library of Congress Cataloging-in-Publication Data is available.

ISBN 0-471-42977-5

Printed in the United States of America.

10 9 8 7 6 5 4 3

Computer Manual in MATLAB
to Accompany
Pattern Classification

Second Edition

Contents

Preface

The MATLAB classification toolbox was started by Elad Yom-Tov as a course assignment in Ron Meir's graduate course on Pattern Classification at the Technion. It has been expanded greatly and altered so as to accompany the textbook **Pattern Classification** (2nd ed.) by R. O. Duda, P. E. Hart and D. G. Stork. As such, it contains all algorithms in the text, and to the extent possible uses its terminology and notation. The code has been used in beta form in over 30 courses worldwide, and has been improved from numerous comments and bug fixes. Nevertheless, we would appreciate any suggestions through the contact information given on `http://www.rii.ricoh.com/~stork/DHS.html`.

We thank Hilt Serby, Igor Mackienco and Viktor Usaf for coding assistance and Martin Boliek for help with Framemaker.

We wish you the best of luck in your studies and research!

David G. Stork
Elad Yom-Tov

CHAPTER 1

Introduction to MATLAB

MATLAB (from "matrix laboratory") is a language and environment for technical computing designed to handle large data sets and matrix operations easily and efficiently; as such it is well suited to problems in signal processing, statistical estimation, and especially pattern classification. This chapter will provide a basic introduction to the MATLAB language, mathematical operations, definitions of variables and so forth needed for use of the algorithms in **Pattern Classification** (2nd ed.). The only pre-requisites are a familiarity with programming such as Fortran, C, C++, Java, Mathematical, and so on. There are a number of excellent introduction such as MATLAB manuals from The Mathworks® or from independent writers, listed in the References, that go well beyond the material presented here.

The full MATLAB system consists of:

- *MATLAB language*: MATLAB is a high-level language optimized for matrix and array operations and contains a number of features found in object-oriented languages.

- *Working environment*: The working environment contains a number of tools for managing programs, debugging and more.

- *Handle Graphics*®: This is the graphics component of the overall system and contains both high-level commands for graphing, data visualization and basic image processing, as well as low-level commands for building graphical user interfaces (GUIs).

- *Mathematical function library*: This library contains a number of files implementing broadly applicable algorithms such as Fourier transforms, matrix inversion, and ordinary differential equations. These are organized in directories within the *MATLAB toolbox*.

- *Application Program Interface (API)*: The API is a library of routines that permit you to link your MATLAB code with C and Fortran programs.

We begin with a tour of basic terms and operations, and turn in Chapter 2 to functions, structure and programming. Novices might wish to run MATLAB while reading the following, which can be considered a short "guided tour" and does not require the classification toolbox introduced in Chapter 3.

Basic navigation and interaction

Once MATLAB has been installed on your machine and invoked, you will be given a command window with a prompt: ». Type `ctrl-c` at any time to interrupt processing and `quit` at any time to exit. MATLAB is an interpreted language, meaning that you enter commands or programs which do not need to be compiled. That is, you type in a command at the prompt, hit `return`, and the answer is computed and displayed, for instance:

```
»7 + 3

ans =

    10
```

If no output variable has been specified, the answer is labelled `ans`. You can assign values to variables as follows:

```
»a = 9


a =



    9
```

Depending upon your system, you should be able to scroll using up-arrow and down-arrow keys, accessing previous line. Thus if you hit the *up-arrow*, you'll return to the first entry, 7 + 3, which then appears on the current prompt line and can be run again.

Scalars, variables and basic arithmetic

Just as you saw, scalar variables are assigned as:

```
»b = 25
```

```
b =
```

```
    25
```

Variables hold their values throughout a MATLAB session until you re-assign them. You can examine the variables (and functions, below) by the command whos and also re-assign them or clear an individual variable, for instance with clear, or by clear all. Thus if a and b have not been cleared, you can perform the following simple computation:

```
»a - b
```

```
ans =
```

```
    -16
```

The simple arithmetic operators are denoted +, −, * and /, as:

```
»3 * a
```

```
ans =
```

```
27
```

Infinity is represented by inf, and an undefined value is returned as NaN, or "not a number," as in:

```
»0/0
```

```
Warning: Divide by zero.
```

```
ans =
```

```
NaN
```

There are several constants of use in pattern classification, in particular π (pi) and $i = $ i or j for $\sqrt{-1}$.

Relational and logical operators

The six fundamental relational operators are <, =, >, >=, ==, and ~= (for not equal to); the logical operators are & (and), | (or) and ~ (not). The logical values true and false are represented by 1 and 0. Thus examples of logical tests are:

```
»5 == 3+2
```

```
ans =
```

```
1
```

that is, true. Similarly,

```
»(2 >= 3) & (1 == 1)
```

```
ans =


    0
```

that is, `false`.

Lists, vectors and matrices

Square brackets enclose lists and matrices; commas are delimiters for rows, and semicolons are delimiters for columns. A column vector is a d-by-1 matrix, while a row vector a 1-by-d matrix. There is no simple provision in MATLAB for bold typefont, which might help us distinguish scalars from vectors and matrixes; upper- and lower-case symbols and names (except for some special MATLAB internal names) can be used for any of these mathematical objects. Nevertheless, in this manual and associated software we shall generally use lower-case letters and all-lower-case names for scalars and upper-case letters for lists vectors, matrixes. Early versions of MATLAB separated elements in lists (or row vectors) by simple spaces, later versions separate elements with a comma, the convention we use here:

```
»Data = [5, 7, 9.1, -4, 3.6]


Data =


    5.0000    7.0000    9.1000   -4.0000    3.6000
```

Since rows are separated by semicolons, you define a column vector as follows:

```
»A = [5; 6; 7]


A =
```

```
    5

    6

    7
```

Vector addition and subtraction are denoted by + and −, for instance

```
»A + [2; 0; -6]
```

```
ans =
```

```
    7

    6

    1
```

You can access the component of a vector by parentheses,

```
»A(2)
```

```
ans =
```

```
    6
```

Another useful way is to access components of a list or matrix is to use `find`, which returns the indexes for a condition. For example,

```
»find(A > 3)
ans =
```

```
    1    2
```

that is, the indexes in the list A whose values are greater than 3 are indexes 1 and 2.

The inner product or "dot" product of a row and a column vector is denoted *

```
»[1, 0, 4] * [5; 3; 9]
```

```
ans =
```

```
     41
```

Of course, the dimensions of vectors (and matrices, below) must match for addition, subtraction as well as inner and outer products, otherwise the error message "Matrix dimensions must agree" will be returned.

The transpose of a vector or matrix is indicated by a single apostrophe or single quote, for instance B', or explicitly

```
»[5; 9; 1]'
```

```
ans =
```

```
     5     9     1
```

A matrix uses a simple comma (or a simple space) as a delimiter between elements within in a row, and the semicolon between rows themselves, as

```
»C = [ 1, 2, 3; 4, 5, 6; 7, 8, 9]
```

```
C =
```

```
     1     2     3
     4     5     6
     7     8     9
```

Matrix multiplication

The general matrix product $C = AB$ requires the column dimension of A to be equal to the row dimension of B. (Additionally, the product is defined if one or both of them are scalars.) Of course, if A is m-by-n and B is n-by-r, then their product C is m-by-r.

First we assign some matrices:

```
»A = [3, 4, 5; 1, 2, 3]

A =

        3        4        5
        1        2        3
```

```
»B = [1, 2; 4, 5; 3, 9]

B =

        1        2
        4        5
        3        9
```

The matrix product can be computed simply

```
»A*B

ans =
```

```
        34      71

        18      39
```

This product can all be written explicitly as code, our first simple program:

```
»for i=1:2

    for j = 1:2

        C(i,j) = A(i,:)*B(:,j);

    end

end
```

You can check that this yields the same correct answer as found above:

```
»C


C =


        34      71

        18      39
```

This is our first multi-line program, so it pays to take a moment to understand how MATLAB processes it. After you've typed in the first line, MATLAB performs syntactic analysis to see that this line, taken alone, is not a valid program, and thus allows you to enter more lines. As we shall see in Chapter 2, one form of process loop is denoted `for... end`, and the colon denotes increments, with the default increment 1. In some versions of MATLAB, these function words are color coded in the command window so you can more easily read and understanding the code. Note that the central line of this program computes a dot product between two vectors, a row vector `A(i,:)` and the column vector `B(:,j)`, and as such invokes an implicit loop over the free indexes.

Matrix multiplication is not commutative, that is, except in unusual cases **AB** does not equal **BA**. A matrix can be multiplied on the right by a column vector and on the left by a row vector. Of course, the dimensions must match.

```
»A*[5; 2; 8]
```

```
ans =
```

```
    63

    33
```

A useful matrix is the square *n*-by-*n* identity matrix, denoted eye(n)

```
»eye(3)
```

```
ans =
```

```
    1      0      0

    0      1      0

    0      0      1
```

Vector and matrix norms

The *p*-norm of a vector X,

$$\|x\|_p = \left(\Sigma |x_i|^p\right)^{1/p}$$

is computed by norm(X,p). If the value of *p* is not referenced, then the default is *p=2*, giving the Euclidean norm:

```
»X = [3, 4]
```

```
X =
```

```
        3       4


»norm(X)


ans =


        5
```

Determinants, inverses and pseudoinverses

The determinant of a square matrix is denoted det ( ), for instance

```
»D = [1, 4; 2, 10]


D =


        1       4
        2      10


»det(D)


ans =


        2
```

Likewise, the inverse of a non-singular matrix is computed as:

```
»inv(D)


ans =


    5.0000   -2.0000

   -1.0000    0.5000
```

If a matrix **E** is not square, then neither its determinant nor inverse are defined. Nevertheless, we can seek the solution matrix **X** for the equations **EX = I** or **XE = I**, where **I** is the identity matrix. This solution is the Moore-Penrose pseudoinverse, and is computed with `pinv(E)`.

```
»E = [1, 2, 4; 2, 0, 2]


E =


     1     2     4

     2     0     2


»pinv(E)


ans =


   -0.1765    0.4706

    0.2353   -0.2941

    0.1765    0.0294
```

You can check that the pseudoinverse is correct:

```
»E*pinv(E)


ans =


        1.0000    0.0000
             0    1.0000
```

Matrix powers and exponentials

A square matrix **F** can be raised to a power p, where p must be a positive integer.

```
»F = [1, 2; 4, 3]


F  =


        1      2
        4      3


»F^2


ans =


        9      8
       16     17
```

If **F** is square and nonsingular, then `F^(-p)` is equivalent to `(inv(F))^p`.

```
»F^(-2)
```

```
ans =
```

```
    0.6800    -0.3200
   -0.6400     0.3600
```

We can also computer an element-by-element powers, where the period (.) is requred, as

```
»Y = F.^2
```

```
Y =
```

```
     1      4
    16      9
```

We shall occasionally take the square root of a matrix with `sqrtm(F)`

```
»sqrtm(F)
```

```
ans =
```

```
    1.0000    1.4142
    2.0000    1.7321
```

which uses a more accurate algorithm than `F^(1/2)`.

Eigenvalues and eigenvectors

A d-by-d (square) non-degenerate matrix **G** has d eigenvectors **v** and associated eigenvalues λ, i.e., those that satisfy $\mathbf{Gv} = \lambda\mathbf{v}$. We let the diagonal matrix $\mathbf{\Lambda}$ contain the eigenvalues and let the columns of matrix **V** contain the eigenvectors. Then the d equations become $\mathbf{GV} = \mathbf{V\Lambda}$, giving the eigenvalue decomposition $\mathbf{G} = \mathbf{V\Lambda V}^{-1}$. We can define a column vector of the eigenvalues of **G** as follows:

```
»G = [1, 0, 4; 0, 2, 0; 4, 0, 1]


G =


        1       0       4

        0       2       0

        4       0       1


»Lambda = eig(G)


Lambda =


    2.0000

   -3.0000

    5.0000
```

The same function with two output arguments yields the eigenvectors in a diagonal matrix:

```
»[V, D] = eig(G)


V =
```

```
         0       0.7071       0.7071

    1.0000            0            0

         0      -0.7071       0.7071


D =


    2.0000            0            0

         0      -3.0000            0

         0            0       5.0000
```

Data analysis

It is often simplest to treat data in columns:

```
»Data = [1, 5, 4; 2, -4, 6; -3, 5, 5; 3, 4, 9]


Data =


     1      5      4

     2     -4      6

    -3      5      5

     3      4      9
```

Basic statistical functions such as the maximum, minimum, standard deviation, and so on are computed in each column, as:

```
»max(Data)
```

```
ans =

       3       5       9

»min(Data)

ans =

      -3      -4       4

»std(Data)

ans =

   2.6300    4.3589    2.1602
```

Some of the most useful data analysis functions, applied to a list, are given in Table 1. These functions take as arguments lists or matrices.

TABLE 1. Basic data analysis functions, applied to a list

Function	Description
max	largest component
min	smallest component
mean	mean or average
median	median
std	standard deviation
sum	sum of elements
cumsum	cumulative sum of elements
diff	difference between successive elements
sort	sort elements in ascending order

A particularly useful function in pattern classification is the covariance of a data set:

```
»Data2 = [1, 1; -1, -1; 0, .5; 0, -.5]


Data2 =


    1.0000    1.0000

   -1.0000   -1.0000

         0    0.5000

         0   -0.5000


»cov(Data2)
```

```
ans =


     0.6667      0.6667

     0.6667      0.8333
```

Furthermore, the correlation coefficient is computed as

```
»corrcoef(Data2)
```

```
ans =


     1.0000      0.8944

     0.8944      1.0000
```

Clearing variables and functions

You saw above how to clear a specific variable by the `clear` command, for instance `clear b`. Likewise you can clear a specific function, or all functions, or all functions and variables by the following calls, respectively:

```
clear b
clear functions
clear all
```

Data types

MATLAB handles six fundamental data types or classes: `double`, `char`, `sparse`, `uint8`, `cell`, and `struct`, each of which can appear in two-dimensional versions or matrices. You assign the data type as listed in Table 2.

TABLE 2. Data types

Class	Example	Description

`double`	`7.9`
	`[4, 2; 3.9, -6]`
	`4+2i`
		double precision numeric array

`char`	`'Pattern'`	string or character list
`sparse`	`speye(3)`	sparse double precision matrix in two-dimensions
`cell`	`{49 'recogni-tion' eye(5)}`	cell array; elements contain other arrays, possibly of different type
`struct`	`a.color = 'green';` `a.mat = eye(4)`	structured array, have field names; the fields contain other arrays
`uint8`	`uint8(eye(4))`	unsigned 8 bit integer array, containing integers from 0 to 255

The classification toolbox uses `double` and `char` (for string operations) and occassionally `sparse`. The 8-bit unsigned integer or `uint8` type is particularly useful for representing pixel images and image processing.

With these basics we turn in the next chapter to multi-line programs and calling MATLAB routines.

CHAPTER 2

Programming in MATLAB

In the last chapter we saw a very simple multi-line program for multiplying matrices. In general, however, program code is not written in the command window but instead written and stored in so-called *M-files* for easy re-use and debugging. M-files are called from the command window and even from other M-files, as we shall see. Actually, there are two uses of M-files: *scripts* (that merely execute statements but do not return values) and *functions* (that accept input arguments and return output values). In this chapter we illustrate the writing, calling and debugging of code in M-files, as well as the creation and use of data files. In Chapter 3 we will consider the function algorithms in the classification toolbox, which are all stored in such M-files.

We start with a quick example of a script to draw a graph of a specific Gaussian distribution, then turn to functions. You can edit an existing M-file by merely opening the file, or by typing `edit <filename>` (e.g., `edit Gaussian` for the file `Gaussian.m`) in the command line. Alternatively you create a new one by opening a the text editor by clicking the *New M-file* button in the menu bar of your command window. M-files for both scripts and functions have names that must end in the extension `.m`. It is convenient to keep your M-files in folders organized by the general use.

Scripts

Click on the *New M-file* button on your command window and type the following code in the new window:

```
% An M-file script to draw a unit-variance Gaussian

x = -4:0.1:4        % creates a list of x values

y = 1/sqrt(2 * pi) * exp(-x.^2/2) % computes y values

plot(x,y,'-')

title('Unit-variance Gaussian')
```

Close and save your file, naming it MyGaussPlot.m. Now in the command window, type MyGaussPlot and hit return. You should see a plot such as the following:

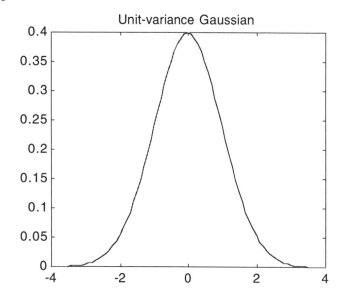

FIGURE 1. The output of MyGaussPlot.m.

The first line of any script is a comment, and must begin with a %. The rest of the script contains the code. This M-file itself calls another M-file, plot.m, provided with MATLAB.

Functions

M-files for functions take in arguments as inputs and return output values; these files have a four-part structure:

1. A *function definition line*, which gives the function name as well as the order of input and output arguments

2. An *H1 line*, or "help 1" line, which contains text and other notes to describe the function returned when you use a lookfor call to seek help.

3. *Help text*, which is text to describe the function. The H1 line, help lines, and other comments must be proceeded by the comment delimiter %.

4. The *function body*, which contains the code to compute the function.

As above, create a new M-file, here called MyGaussian.m containing the following code:

```
function y = MyGaussian(x,mu,sigma)

% MyGaussian computes a one-dimensional Gaussian

% MyGaussian(x,mu,sigma) returns the value at x of a
normalized Gaussian centered on mu with standard devia-
tion sigma

y = 1/sqrt(2*pi*sigma) * exp(-(x-mu)^2/(2*sigma^2))
```

Close, save, and name your file MyGaussian.m. Now you can invoke your function in your command window:

```
»MyGaussian(2,1,4)


y =


    0.1933
```

```
ans =
```

```
    0.1933
```

You can check on a function by typing `lookfor`, which returns your H1 line:

```
»lookfor MyGaussian
```

```
 MyGaussian computes the one-dimensional Gaussian
```

If you need to edit your function, you can open the file directly, or call a text editor from the command line as:

```
»edit MyGaussian
```

which will open the file `MyGaussian.m`. A useful utility is invoked by `what` on the command line, which yields a list of the names of M-files in the current directory.

The first function called in an M-file is called the primary function but an M-file can contain additional functions, or subfunctions, which are accessed only by the functions within the M-file itself.

Flow control

The six flow control structures in MATLAB programs are

- `if...else` or `if...elseif`: executes the intervening code if the logical statement evaluates to `true`
- `switch...case` or `switch...otherwise`: evaluates different sets of statements determined by a logical condition
- `while`: executes a set of statements repeatedly, based on a logical condition
- `for`: executes statements a fixed number of times
- `try...catch`: executes the statements until an error occurs
- `return`: exits the loop or control structure

All of these structures are terminated with an end statement.

if... else, if... elseif

The general form of this statement is

```
if logical_expression

    statements

end
```

If the `logical_expression` statement evaluates to 1 (`true`), then all the statements between `if` and `end` are executed; if the `if` evaluates to 0 (`false`), then none are. The `elseif` further restricts the logical tests:

```
if logical_expression1

    statements1

elseif logical_experssion2

    statements2

        .

        .

        .

else

    statementsn

end
```

The `elseif` conditions are tested in sequence until first one evaluates to `true`. Then only the corresponding statements are executed and the control structure exited.

switch

The general form of this statement is

```
switch expression
      case value1
             statements1
      case value2
             statements2
          .
          .
          .
      otherwise
             statmentsn
end
```

If the *expression* evaluates to value1, then all the statements1 are executed; if *expression* evaluates to value2, then all the statements2 are executed, and so on. If *expression* does not match any of the cases, *statementsn* are executed. The sequence of cases is important. As in the if...elseif control structure, the first case where the expression matches a value is executed and none others, even if these subsequent statements might also match.

while

The general form of this statement is

```
while expression
      statements
end
```

A while loop executes as long as the *expression* is valid, though it can be broken at any time using the break or return statement.

for

The general form of this statement is

```
for index = start:increment:end

        statements
end
```

If no increment is specified, the default is *increment* = 1. Although the for structure can be useful, MATLAB is optimized for vectorized processing and thus many for loops should be recast in their vectorized forms. Thus a simple for loop such as

```
j = 0;
for t = 0:0.1:10
     j = j+1;
     y(j) = cos(t);
end
```

is far less efficient that the following vectorized form:

```
t = 0:0.1:10
y = cos(t)
```

try...catch

The general form of this statement is

```
try
```

```
    statement1

    statement2

        .

        .

        .

catch

end
```

These are executed in sequence until an error occurs, such as division by zero, collision of data types, and so on.

return

The `return` statement merely returns control to the keyboard.

User input

MATLAB code can be used in an interactive mode, where processing halts until the user provides a requested value, as in:

```
x = input('prompt_string')
```

For instance, you could eliminate the parameters in the call to MyGaussian.m but then include code in the M-file that ask for use input such as

```
mu = input('input the mean')

sigma = input('enter the standard deviation')
```

and so on. If the input is to be a string, the request line needs to indicate the string data type, as for instance

```
MyTitle = input('Enter the title', 's')
```

where the 's' indicates the input is typed as a string.

It is occasionally useful to pause processing, particularly when debugging, so the user can see an intermediate result. This is accomplished by the statement

```
pause(n)
```

where n is the number of seconds.

Debugging

Debugging invokes a separate debugging window, and is best explained by an example. As above, create an M-file called MyMedian.m that is to calculate the median of an input vector X as shown:

```
function y = MyMedian(X)

% computes median of a list X

% computes the median of a list, i.e., the value for
which half of the entries are higher, half lower.  If
the number of elements in the list is odd, then the
median is the middle element in the ordered list.  If
instead the number of elements in the list is even, the
median is the mean of the two central values

 Y = sort(X)      % sorts the list

 if length(X)/2 == round(length(X)/2 - 0.5)    % even
number of elements

 y = (Y(length(X)/2) + Y(length(X)/2 + 1))/2

 else  % odd number of elements

 y = Y(round(length(X)/2)+1)    % note:  this is an error
end
```

Notice that if X has an odd number of elements, the above code computes the incorrectly. Test your program from the command line:

```
»X = [3, 12, 2, 9, 5]
```

```
X =

    3    12     2     9     5
»MyMedian(X)

Y =

    2     3     5     9    12

l =

    5

y =

    9

ans =

    9
```

Note the error: the median should instead be 5.

MATLAB's debugger can be has a number of debugging techniques. Here is one
way to debug your code. Set a breakpoint, for instance on the line `l =
length(X)`.  Then re-run `MyMedian.m` from the command line.

```
»MyMedian(X)


Y =


        2        3        5        9       12


1 =


        5


K>>
```

The execution stops at the breakpoint and the prompt K>> shows you are in keyboard mode. You can examine the values of variables, for instance the sorted list Y from the command window:

```
K>>Y =


        2        3        5        9       12



K>>
```

There's no problem up to that line, so go to the debugger, place your cursor on the line with the breakpoint and then remove the breakpoint by means of the pulldown menu. As before, now set a new breakpoint at the line y = Y((1+1)/2 + 1) and run the program again from the command line.

```
K>>MyMedian(X)
```

```
Y =

     2     3     5     9    12

l =

     5

y =

     9

ans =

     9


K>>
```

Now you can see the error in the calculation for the case of an odd number of elements. Open and edit MyMedian.m to change the function. Re-run from the command line.

There are a number of other ways to debug, such as single stepping, which are described in MATLAB manuals.

Data, and file input and output

Data is stored in files with the extension `.dat` which can contain no functional code.

To open a file from the command line a use file `fopen`, and `fclose`.

```
»fid = fopen('filename','permission')
```

where `fid` is file identifier, and `permission` can take on four possible values, `'r'` (read only), `'w'` (write only), `'a'` (append to only) and `'r+'` (read and write). For instance

```
»fid = fopen('myoutput.dat','w')
```

opens or creates the file `myoutput.dat` for writing only. Close the file by typing

```
»fclose myoutput.dat
```

You can close *all* files by `status = fclose('all')`. Finally, you can find the M-files in the current directory by typing `what`.

Data files typically end in `.dat` and are written as output of a MATLAB program.

Strings

An array of characters is a string, and must be placed inside single quotes, for example

```
»mystring = 'here is a string'


mystring =


here is a string
```

Strings can occur in two-dimensional arrays,

```
mylist = ['here is a string'; 'here is another string']
```

Note that both rows must have the same number of characters. It is traditional to "pad" entries with blanks so that they have the same number of characters. Alternatively, you can use `char`, which pads the ends of strings with blanks so that each entry has the same number of characters.

Operations on strings

The function `strcmp` (for string comparison) determines whether two full strings are identical:

```
»str1 = 'abcddd'
»str2 =  'abcdef'
»strcmp(str1,str2)
```

```
ans =
```

```
     0
```

The function `strncmp`, which takes three arguments, determines whether the first n characters (the prefix of length n) of the two strings are equal:

```
»strncmp(str1,str2,3)
```

```
ans =
```

```
     1
```

that is, `true`. Likewise we have

```
»strncmp(str1,str2,5)
```

```
ans =
```

```
        0
```

You compare equal-length strings, character-by-character, with the equality opera-
tor. The output is a list with a 1 or a 0, depending whether the corresponding characters match or not.

CHAPTER 3

Classification toolbox

This chapter describes how to load and use the classification toolbox, including its Graphical User Interface (GUI). The toolbox contains a set of algorithms, implemented in MATLAB M-files, data files, and more.

The general types of files in the classification toolbox are:

- Control routines for the Graphical User Interface (e.g., `classifier`)
- Preprocessing and feature selection algorithms (e.g., `whitening_transform`)
- Error estimation methods (e.g., `Chernoff`)
- Clustering algorithms (e.g., `k-means`)
- Single parametric classification algorithms (e.g., `Perceptron`)
- Meta algorithms that can be used when training (e.g., `Ada_Boost`)
- Housekeeping/utilities, which the user will rarely if ever call directly (e.g., `process_params`)
- Data sets, in files which end in `.mat` (e.g., `Ch5CompEx` for the data in the text's Chapter 5 Computer Exercises)

We shall begin by loading the toolbox and a simple example, then turn to more general use.

Loading the toolbox and starting MATLAB

The classification toobox is available from the Wiley site:

http://www.wiley.com/WileyCDA/WileyTitle/productCd-0471056693.html.

Use the password: Z49K1Q82RN fill in the form.

Once you have downloaded the toolbox, follow the below steps:

1. Create a new directory on your home machine, preferably under the MATLAB directory.
2. Unzip the contents of the toolbox zip file into this new directory.
3. Include the path of the new directory in the MATLAB search path by typing in the command window: `addpath` *<directory>*

Graphical User Interface

The easiest way to operate the classification toolbox is via the graphic user interface (GUI). Launch MATLAB and then start the GUI by typing `classifier` at the prompt in the command window. This will bring up a screen as shown in Figure 1.

We shall consider the GUI in greater depth below, but here give a brief overview. At the left, the File name box and its button, is for entering data files. The box below is for specifying preprocessing and the classification algorithm itself, via a pulldown menu. There are three methods for estimating the error of the trained classifier: Holdout, Cross-validation and Resubstitution. If appropriate, the number of redraws specifies how many times a given data set will be resampled for estimating the error. There are a number of data preprocessing algorithms, the default being None. The classification algorithms are selected from a pulldown menu, with LS (for Least-squares linear classifier) being the default.

Other ways to enter data are provided by the box below containing control buttons. For some distributions, such as Gaussian data entered by hand, the Bayes decision regions can be calculated and displayed, as selected by the button at the left. The remaining boxes are for displaying messages and classification error rates.

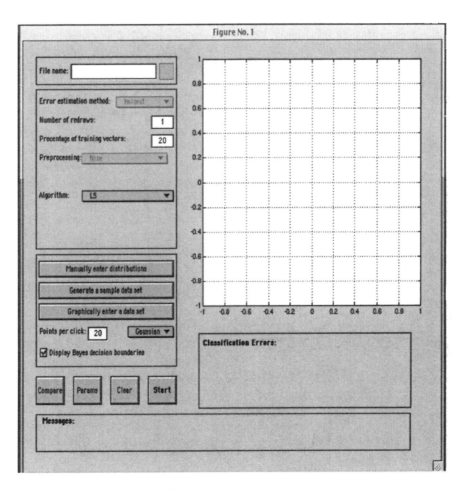

FIGURE 1. The toolbox GUI window.

Introductory examples

Begin the first example by entering the data set clouds, either by typing clouds in the File name window box or by clicking on the adjacent button and selecting clouds.mat. Next, check that the **Display Bayes decision boundaries button** is selected. Then click on the **Start** button at the bottom. After a few moments your GUI should look like

Figure 2. With the above operations you have loaded the distribution file `clouds.m` into the workspace and classified it using a linear least-squares classifier (LS), trained on 20% of the data and tested on the remaining 80% via a holdout method, as listed as default parameters visible in the windows.

Because this dataset the underlying distribution components are Gaussian, the toolbox algorithms can compute and display the Bayes decision boundaries as well as the Bayes error. The classification error on the test data and training data are shown at the lower right.

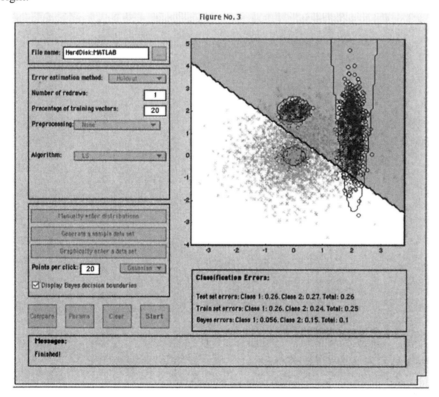

FIGURE 2. The linear and Bayes decision boundaries for the clouds classification problem.

Now try another example. First hit the **Clear** button near the bottom to clear the workspace and other spaces.

This time enter data graphically, as follows. Click the **Graphically enter a data set** button. The pulldown menu and **Points per click** window show that you will enter 20 points in a Gaussian distribution per click. Right-click (or simply click) and drag a region within the graph area; 20 points randomly chosen from a Gaussian distribution for category 0 appear. Now left-click (or option-click) and drag to produce 20 points for category 1. Choose Nearest_Neighbor classifier from the pulldown menu, and enter 1 to specify the *k=1* nearest-neighbor classifer. Now click the **Start** button. After a few moments you should see a figure such as in Figure 3, though of course the details will differ because of your particular sets of data points.

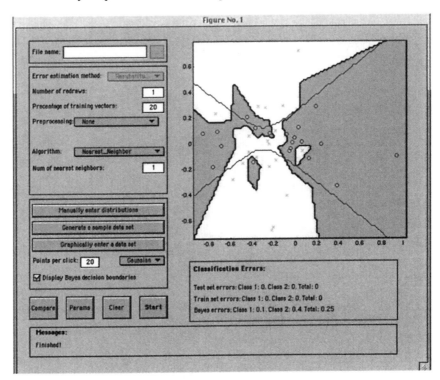

FIGURE 3. The k=1 nearest-neighbor and Bayes decision boundaries for two Gaussian distributions entered graphically.

In many cases decision boundaries are plotted using MATLAB's internal contour graphics routines. As such, linear decision segments may appear as rippled (according to the sampling resolution) as in Figure 3, rather than straight.

You may wish to explore the toolbox and GUI by chosing different data sets, classification algorithms and so forth before reading further.

GUI controls

Now that we have seen two simple examples, we turn to a general description of the GUI. The general control and output regions of the GUI are:

- Input file box
- Classification and preprocessing parameters box
- Parametric distribution box
- Command buttons
- System messages box
- Error percentages box
- Graphics area

Many of the functions can also be selected from the pulldown menu on the toolbar at the top of the MATLAB window.

Input file box

Training data from files is input through the input file box, either by explicit name of the file (without adding the .mat suffix), or via the button. In some cases MATLAB might not find the path to a data file, and thus you must use the button. For a general classification problem, you may need to create your .mat file, usually by writing the file from MATLAB or another application, as we shall see below.

Classification and preprocessing parameters box

The Classification and preprocessing parameters box contains pulldown menus for the different algorithms in the toolbox, as well as new ones you might add, as described on page 61. Some of the algorithms have additional parameters that can be entered by a new window that appears once that algorithm is selected. For instance, if you choose Nearest_Neighbor algorithm, a window marked **Num of nearest neighbors** appears, containing the default value of 3 nearest neighbors, which you can change to any integer greater than 0.

Likewise, the preprocessing algorithm is chosen via a pulldown menu. Some preprocessing algorithms require you to specify additional parameters. For instance, if you choose PCA (for principle component analysis), a window marked **New data dimension** appears, containing the default value of 2 dimensions which you can change to any dimension between 1 and the dimensionality of the training data itself. You can use the Options menu to preprocess each class separately.

The Error estimation method is similarly specified by a pulldown menu. For instance, in Cross_Validation the error is estimated by resampling the data set; the **Number of redraws** box specifies the (selectable) number of times a random set of patterns is drawn from the data. The **Percentage of training vectors** must be between 0 and 100, with 20 a useful default value.

Parametric distribution box

The parametric distribution box allows you to enter data drawn from distributions such as a Gaussian or uniform distribution.

Command buttons

The four command buttons are

1. **Compare** launches a new GUI for comparing several classification algorithms (See "Classifier comparisons" on page 59 below.)
2. **Params** opens a window for inspecting and specifying classification parameters
3. **Clear** empties the workspace and output boxes, including the graphics area
4. **Start** initiates preprocessing and classification

System messages box

This box displays error messages, messages showing the state of ongoing computations, and so on.

Error percentages box

This box displays the classification errors, and, if available, the Bayes error rate. The classification errors are estimated according to the method selected in the pulldown menu:

1. Holdout (the default option): This trains the classifier using the percentage of points specified in the window below, and all other points for testing.

2. Cross-validation: This divides the data into subsets, the number of which is determined by the integer in the **Number of redraws** box.

3. Resubstitution: This trains and tests the classifier using all the points.

If the Holdout or Resubstitution method is used, and more than one redraw specified, the classifier will be trained a number of times and the error reported is the average of the individual estimates.

Graphics area

The two-dimensional graphics area can be used for input (using the **Graphically enter a data set** button) and output, for displaying data points, decision boundaries and decision regions.

Creating your own data files

Training and test data reside in files such as `clouds.mat` and if you create your own such files, they must conform to a particular structure. Data sets are stored as two variables:

1. `patterns`: This is a d-by-n matrix, where d is the number of dimensions of the data and n the number of examples. If $d>2$, a feature selection GUI will open and request the user preprocess the data to yield two-dimensional data to be compatible with the display.

2. `targets`: This is a 1-by-n vector containing the category labels. It is traditional for a two-category problem to use the labels 0 and 1.

Random data can also be represented as distributions, in particular, mixtures of k Gaussian components. This structure is described in Table 1.

TABLE 1. **Representation of distribution parameters**

Name	Symbol	Dimensions	Description
Mu	μ	$p \times d$	d-dimensional means of the p components
sigma	Σ	$p \times d \times d$	d-by-d dimensional covariances matrices of the p components
w	$\mathbf{w}$	$1 \times p$	the relative weights of the p components, constrained such that $\sum_{i=1}^{p} w_i = 1$.
P	$P(\omega_i)$	scalar	Prior probability of the category

Data file can be created in several ways. The easiest is using the **Graphically enter a dataset** option, described above. Another method is to design a parametric distribution comprising of Gussian and uniform distributions entered explicitly through a dialog box. To do this press the **Manually enter distributions** button on the GUI. The toolbox will ask you to enter the number of distributions (Number of Gaussians and uniform distributions) for each class, as well as the prior probability of each class. (The default is one distribution per class, and equal probabilities.) Then, a GUI will prompt you to enter the paramters of each distribution as well as its relative weight in the class. When you finish, press **OK**. You have not generated a distribution; instead, the parameters of the distribution are in a structure called distribution_parameters.

You can also create a distribution structure through the text interface. For example, the following code will generate a distribution with one Gaussian in class 0, and two uniform distributions in class 1. The priors are 0.66 for class 1, and the two uniform distributions are of equal probabilities.

```
distribution_parameters(1).p = 0.33;

distribution_parameters(1).mu = [0, 0];

distribution_parameters(1).sigma(1,:,:) = [1, 0; 0, 1];

distribution_parameters(1).type = 'Gaussian';

distribution_parameters(1).w = 1;

distribution_parameters(2).p = 0.66;
```

```
distribution_parameters(2).mu = [-1, -2; 4, 1];

distribution_parameters(2).sigma(1,:,:) = [1, 0; 0, 0];

distribution_parameters(2).sigma(2,:,:) = [0.5, 0.5; 0, 0];

distribution_parameters(2).type(1) = 'Uniform';

distribution_parameters(2).type(2) = 'Uniform';

distribution_parameters(2).w = [0.5; 0.5];
```

In order to generate points for this distribution, press the **Generate a sample dataset** button, which will prompt you for the number of point to be generated, and then generate a sample distribution from the distribution you have now created. You can save your distribution (parameters and points) by selecting the Save option from the File menu.

The methods described above make it possible to generate two-dimensional, two-class distributions. You can generate distributions with more classes and/or more dimensions through the text interface. For example, by typing the following, you will create a distribution with three dimensions and four classes (with labels 0 through 3):

```
patterns=[0, -1, 2.4, 6.1; 3, 5, -1.9, -9.8; 1.2, 7.3, -9.1,
0.1];

targets=[0, 1, 2, 3];
```

Classifying using the text-based interface

You can classify data through the MATLAB command window. This is particularly useful and even essential when the data are not two-dimensional, or involve discrete attributes rather than real-valued vector features.

In this example, you will use a least-squares linear classifier (LS) in conjunction with AdaBoost boosting method on half of 5000 points from the clouds data, using the other half of the data to estimate the error.

1. To load the data, type: load clouds. This statement assigns the vector patterns to the the corresponding vector in the clouds dataset.

2. To build the classifier, type (with no spaces): `test_targets=` `Ada_Boost(patterns(:,1:2500),targets(1,2500),` `pat-` `terns(:,2501:end),'[100,''LS'',[]]');` This defines the vector `test_targets` to be the output of the function `Ada_Boost`. Different classification methods have different arguments, and here the `Ada_Boost` function has four arguments: 1) a matrix `patterns`, 2) a vector `targets`, 3) the `test_patterns`, which in this example is drawn from the matrix `patterns` itself, and 4) the parameters, which in this case are involve the least-squares linear classifier, LS. These parameters are listed in the Table 3, or can be queried by typing `help Ada_Boost` or `help LS`, as appropriate.

3. To estimate the error, type: `error=mean(targets(2501:end) ~=` `test_targets)`. This statement assigns the scalar estimate `error` to be the mean of the vector of the difference between `targets` and `test_targets`, which was computed in step 2.

For this example, the error should be roughly 24.5%.

Classifier comparisons

Occassionally you will wish to compare the performance of two or more classification algorithms on the same problem. Such comparisons are specified using a second GUI, which is invoked by clicking on the **Compare** button on the classifier GUI, or by typing `multialgorithms` in the MATLAB command window. Doing so will launches the

GUI shown in Figure 4. The meanings of the terms are the same as in the standard classification GUI of Figure 1.

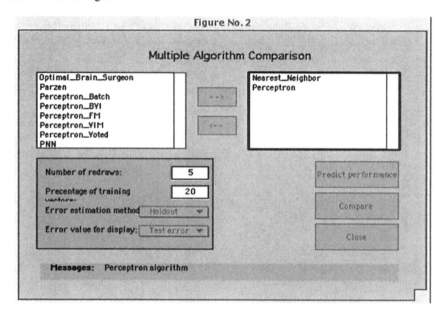

FIGURE 4. The multialgorithm GUI.

Suppose we wish to compare the performance of two or more algorithms on a classification problem. Do this as follows:

1. Close the multialgorithm GUI and launch the standard classifier GUI, as before.
2. Load the data set by typing spirals as the input File name.
3. Press **Compare** button; the multialgorithm GUI will appear.
4. Change the error estimation method to be Holdout, and select Nearest_Neighbor
   and Perceptron classifiers. Train the classifiers with 20 percent of the data and
   choose 5 redraws in the box, as shown in Figure 4.
5. Press **Predict perforamce**.

Your result should be a screen similar to that in Figure 5. Naturally, the linear decision boundary produced by the Perceptron algorithm yields an error of nearly 50% on this difficult highly nonlinear problem.

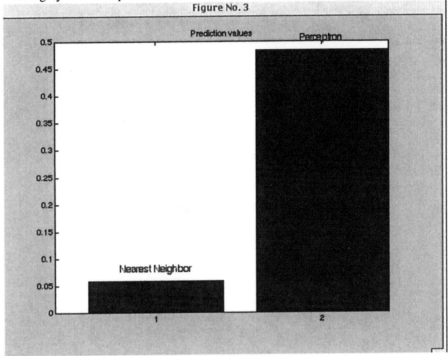

FIGURE 5. The predicted performance of the Nearest-Neighbor and Perceptron algorithms on the sprials classification problem.

How to add new algorithms

The classification toolbox is meant to be a development tool for research and solving practical problems. As such, you may wish to add new preprocessing and classification algorithms to the toolbox.

Adding a preprocessing algorithm

Preprocessing algorithm M-files can have three different structures, determined by the type of output. These formats determine where in the toolbox they must be added.

All algorithms have four inputs: `train_patterns`, `train_targets`, a parameter (or vector of parameters), and a `plot flag`. The value of the `plot flag` (0, 1, 2 or 3) specifies if the user requests plots during training: 0: no plot; 1: plot means (centers) of Gaussians; 2: plot centers of Voronoi cells; 3: plot both Gaussian means (centers) and centers of Voronoi cells.

Every algorithm has at least two outputs, namely `reduced_patterns` and `reduced_targets`. Several algorithms have additional parameter, which is used to reshape the test patterns, as listed in Table 2.

TABLE 2. Additional outputs for preprocessing algorithms.

Additional output	Example algorithm	line in `start_classify.m`
Matrix (reshaping matrix)	PCA	129
Vector (reshaping vector, reduces feature dimenion to 1)	Fisher	138
None (No reshaping)	k_means	151

Once you have written your new preprocessing algorithm, copy its M-file to the toolbox directory. You must then add a reference line in the file `Preprocessing.txt` of the following form:

<Algorithm name>@*<Caption>*@*<Default Parameters>*@*<Display field>*

where

<Algorithm name> is the name of the algorithm, as well as its M-file

<Caption> is the caption to be displayed near the parameter entry box in the GUI

<Default parameters> are the default values for parameters

<Display field> indicates whether parameters are needed in the algorithm; type 'N' in this field if no parameters are needed, otherwise type any other letter.

You should then describe your algorithm in contents.m.

Adding a new classification algorithm

You can add a new classification algorithm much the same as with a new preprocessing algorithm. Classification algorithm M-files take training_patterns, targets and test_patterns in a manner that may depend upon the algorithm itself. The algorithm returns as output the classified test_targets.

Once you have written your new classification algorithm, copy its M-file to the toolbox directory. You must then add a reference line in Classification.txt file in the following form:

<Algorithm name>@*<Caption>*@*<Default Parameters>*@*<Display field>*

where

<Algorithm name> is the name of the algorithm, as well as its M-file

<Caption> is the caption to be displayed near the parameter entry box in the GUI

<Default parameters> are the default values for parameters

<Display field> indicates whether parameters are needed in the algorithm; type 'N' in this field if no parameters are needed; type 'S' to open a short parameter window in the GUI and 'L' to open a long parameter window whenever this algorithm is invoked.

You should then describe your algorithm in contents.m.

Adding a new feature selection algorithm

You can add a new feature selection algorithm much the same as with a new preprocessing algorithm. Feature selection algorithm M-files take patterns and targets as well as algorithm specific parameters. The algorithm returns as output the data in a lower dimension.

Once you have written your new feature selection algorithm, copy its M-file to the tool-box directory. You must then add a reference line to the `Feature_selection.txt` file in the following form:

<Algorithm name>@*<Caption>*@*<Default Parameters>*@*<Display field>*

where

<Algorithm name> is the name of the algorithm, as well as its M-file

<Caption> is the caption to be displayed near the parameter entry box in the GUI

<Default parameters> are the default values for parameters

<Display field> indicates whether parameters are needed in the algorithm; type 'N' in this field if no parameters are needed, otherwise type any other letter.

You should then describe your algorithm in `contents.m`.

List of functions

The following tables contain the algorithms supplied in the classification toolbox. All classification, clustering and feature selection algorithms take as inputs the matrix `features` and targets are `targets`. The tables show the algorithm name (which is the same as the M-file name), the parameters and their default values, as well as additional outputs, as appropriate. The right-most column lists the section in **Pattern Classification** where the algorithm is first described, and the symbols for the parameters.

You can type `help` or `show_algorithms` to get more information. For instance, `show_algorithms('classification')` will show all the classification algorithms. Likewise `show_algorithms('classification',1)` will also show the default parameters for each algorithm.

TABLE 3. Classification algorithms

Algorithm	Parameter(s)	Default(s)	Additional output(s)	Section
Marginaliza-tion	# of missing features, # of patterns with which to compute the marginal	[1, 10]	$P(\omega_i|\mathbf{x}_g)$	§2.1
Minimum_Cost	Cost matrix $\lambda(\alpha_i|\omega_j)$	[0, 1; 1, 0]		§2.3
NDDF				§2.6
Discrete_Bayes				§2.9
ML				§3.2
ML_diag				§3.2
Gibbs	Division resolution	10		§3.5.3
EM	# of Guassians for ω_1 and for ω_2	[1,1]	Params of Gaussians found	§3.9
Parzen	Normalizing factor for window h	1		§4.3
PNN	Gaussian width h	1		§4.3.5
Nearest_Neighbor	# of nearest neighbors k	3		§4.5.4
RCE	maximum radius λ_{max}	1		§4.8
Perceptron	Maximum # of iterations	500	Perceptron weights	§5.5.1
Perceptron_Batch	Maximum # of iterations, θ, η	[1000, 0.01, 0.01]	Perceptron weights; updates throughout learning	§5.5.1
Balanced_Winnow	# of iterations, α, η	[1000, 2, 0.1]	positive weight vector; negative weight vector	§5.5.3

TABLE 3. Classification algorithms (Continued)

Algorithm	Parameter(s)	Default(s)	Additional output(s)	Section
Perceptron_BVI	Maximum # of iterations, η	[1000, 0.01]	Perceptron weights	§5.5.3
Perceptron_VIM	Maximum # of iterations, b, η	[1000, 0.1, 0.01]	Perceptron weights	§5.5.3
Relaxation_BM	Maximum # of iterations, b, η	[1000, 0.1, 0.1]	Classifier weights	§5.6.1
Relaxation_SSM	Maximum # of iterations, b, η	[1000, 0.1, 0.1]	Classifier weights	§5.6.1
LS	Either None or the weights for each pattern		Classifier weights	§5.8.1
LMS	Maximum # of iterations, θ, η	[1000, 0.1, 0.01]	Updates through-out learning	§5.8.4
Ho_Kashyap	Decision type (Basic/ Modified), Maximum # of iterations, θ, η	['Basic', 1000, 0.1, 0.01]	Classifier weights; Margin	§5.9.1
SVM	Kernel (RBF\Polynomial\Linear\Sigmoid), Kernel; parameters, Solver(Perceptron\Quadprog\Lagrangian), Slack	['RBF', 0.05, 'Perceptron', inf]	SVM coeficients	§5.11
Backpropagation_Batch	n_H, Convergence criterion, η	[5,0.1, 0.1]	Hidden unit weights, Output unit weights, Error during training	§6.3.2

TABLE 3. Classification algorithms (Continued)

Algorithm	Parameter(s)	Default(s)	Additional output(s)	Section
Backpropagation_Stochastic	n_H, Convergence criterion, η	[5,0.1, 0.1]	Hidden unit weights, Output unit weights, Error throughout the training	§6.3.2
Multivariate_ Splines	Spline degree, # of knots	[2, 10]		§6.7
Projection_Pursuit	# of components	4	Components weights, Output unit weights	§6.7
Backpropagation_SM	n_H, Convergence criterion, α, η	[5,0.1, .9,0.1]	Hidden unit weights, Output unit weights, Error throughout the training	§6.8.10
Backpropagation_Quickprop	n_H, Convergence criterion, η, μ	[5,0.1, 0.1, 2]	Hidden unit weights, Output unit weights, Error during training	§6.9.3
Backpropagation_CGD	n_H, Convergence criterion	[5,0.1]	Hidden unit weights, Output unit weights, Error vs. training	§6.9.4
RBF_Network	n_H	6	Hidden unit locations, Output unit weights	§6.10.1

TABLE 3. Classification algorithms (Continued)

Algorithm	Parameter(s)	Default(s)	Additional output(s)	Section
Backpropagation_Recurrent	n_H, Convergence criterion, η	[5,0.1, 0.1]	Unit weights; Error vs. training	§6.10.5
Cascade_Correlation	Convergence criterion, η	[0.1, 0.1]	Hidden unit weights, Output unit weights, Error throughout the training	§6.10.6
Optimal_Brain_Surgeon	n_H, Convergence criterion	[10, 0.1]	Hidden unit weights, Output unit weights, Error during training	§6.11
Deterministic_Boltzmann	# of inputs, # of hidden units, Temperature decrease rate, Type of weak learner, Weak learner parameters	[10,10, 0.99, 'LS',[]]		§7.3.3
Genetic_Algorithm	Type of simple classifier,Target error, # of chromosomes, Fraction of crossovers, Fraction of mutations	['LS',0 .1,10,0 .5,0.1]		§7.5.1
Genetic_Programming	Initial function length, # of generations, Number of solutions	[10,100 ,20]	The best solution found	§7.6
CART	Impurity type, Maximum allowed percentage of impurity at node	['Entro py',1]		§8.3
ID3	# of bins, Node percentage	[5,1]		§8.4.1
C4_5	Node percentage	1		§8.4.2

TABLE 3. Classification algorithms (Continued)

Algorithm	Parameter(s)	Default(s)	Additional output(s)	Section
Ada_Boost	Number of iterations, type of weak lerner, parameters for the weak learner	[100,'S tumps', []]	Errors through the iterations	§9.5.2
Interactive_L earning	# of points, Relative weight	[10, .05]		§9.5.3
ML_II	Maximum # of Gauss-ians	[5,5]		§9.6.4
Bayesian_Mode l_Comparison	Maximum # of Gauss-ians	[5,5]		§9.6.5
Components_wi th_DF	# of components	10	Errors throughout the itera-tions	§9.7.1
Components_wi thout_DF	Components	[('LS') ,('ML') ,('Parz en',1)]	Errors throughout the itera-tions	§9.7.2
Local_Polynom ial	# of test points	10		
Perceptron_FM	Maximum # of itera-tions, Slack	[500, 1]	Perceptron weights	
Perceptron_vo ted	# of perceptrons, Method(Linear, Poly-nomial, Gaussian), Method Parameters	[7,'Lin ear',0. 5]		
Pocket	Maximum number of iterations	500		
RDA	λ	0.4		
Store_Grabbag	# of nearest neighbors k	3		
Stumps				

Table 4 lists the preprocessing algorithms in the toolbox.

TABLE 4.   Preprocessing agorithms

Algorithm	Parameter(s)	Default(s)	Additional output(s)	Section
Whitening_tra nsform				§2.5.2
MultipleDis- criminan- tAnalysis			Weight vec- tor	§3.8.3
NearestNeigh- borEditing				§4.5.5
PCA	New data dimension	2	Reshape martix, Pat- tern aver- ages	§10.13.1
Scaling_trans form			Variance matrix, fea- ture aver- ages	

Table 5 lists the clustering methods in the toolbox.

TABLE 5.   Clustering algorithms

Algorithm	Parameter(s)	Default(s)	Additional output(s)	Section
FishersLin- earDiscrimi- nant				§3.8.2
Deterministic _Annealing	# partitions, Cooling rate	[4,.95]		§7.2.1
Stochastic_SA	# partitions, Cooling rate	[4,.95]		§7.2.2
Deterministic _SA	# partitions, Cooling rate	[4,.95]		§7.2.3
k_means	# of partitions	4		§10.4.3

TABLE 5. Clustering algorithms (Continued)

Algorithm	Parameter(s)	Default(s)	Additional output(s)	Section
fuzzy_k_means	# of partitions	4		§10.4.4
BIMSEC	# of partitions, # of attempts	[4, 1]		§10.8
AGHC	# of partitions, Distance function	[4, 'min']		§10.9.2
Min_Spanning_ Tree	Method (NN/inc), # of output points or difference factor	['NN', 2]		§10.9.2
SOHC	# of partitions	4	The labels given for each of the original patterns	§10.9.3
Competitive_l earning	# of partitions, η	[4, .01]	The labels given for each of the original patterns, Weight matrices	§10.11
Leader_Follow er	Minimum distance, Rate	[0.1, 0.1]	The labels given for each of the original patterns, Weight matrices	§10.11.1
Kohonen_SOFM	# units, Window width $|\Lambda|$	[10, 5]	The labels given for each of the original patterns	§10.14.1
DSLVQ	# of partitions	4		

Table 6 lists the feature selection algorithms in the toolbox.

TABLE 6.   Feature selection algorithms

Algorithm	Parameter(s)	Default(s)	Additional output(s)	Section
PCA	Output dimension	2	Reshape martix, Pattern averages	§10.13.1
NLCA	Output dimension, n_H	[2, 5]		§10.13.2
ICA	Output dimension, Convergence rate	[2,1e-30]	Reshape martix	§10.13.3
MDS	Method (ee/ef/ff), Output dimension, Convergence rate	['ee', 2,0.1]		§10.14
HDR	Output dimension	2		§10.14.2
Exhaustive_Feature_Selection	Output dimension, Classifier, Classifier params	[2,'LS',[]]	The numbers of the selected patterns	
Genetic_Culling	Fraction of groups discarded at each iteration, Output dimension, classifier, classifier params	[0.1,2,'LS',[]]	The numbers of the selected features	
Information_based_selection	Output dimension	2	The numbers of the selected features	
Sequential_Feature_Selection	Type (Forward\Backward), Output dimension, Classifier, Classifier params	['Backward',2,'LS',[]]	The numbers of the selected features	

Table 7 shows the commands for the GUI.

TABLE 7. GUI start commands

program name	description
classifier	runs the single-algorithm GUI
multialgorithms	runs the GUI for multiple classification agorithms
show_algorithms	shows which algorithms are available

Table 8 shows the algorithms for computing error bounds.

TABLE 8. Error bounds

program name	description	Section
Chernoff	Chernoff bound	§2.8.1
Bhattacharyya	Bhattacharyya bound	§2.8.2
Discriminability	discriminability d'	§2.8.3

Table 9 shows the internal commands called by other routines. Users will rarely, if need to call these programs directly.

TABLE 9. Internal commands

program name	description
calculate_error	calculates classification error
classification_error	calculates the classification error for a given decision boundary and a set of patterns and targets
classify_parametric	calculates the classification error for a parametric classifier
calculate_region	calculates the bounding box region for the plot
classifier_commands	processes events from the single-alorithm GUI
click_points	manually enter points into the workspace
enter_distribution_commands	

TABLE 9. Internal commands (Continued)

program name	description
feature_selection	
feature_selection_com mands	deals with commands generated by the feature selection module
FindParameters	
FindParametersFunc- tions	
GaussianParameters	
generate_data_set	generates a new data set given its Gaussian parameters
high_histogram	computes the histogram for high-dimensional data
load_file	loads a file containing either data points or distribution parameters or both
make_a_draw	select a number of indices out of the maximum possible
multialgorithms_comma nds	processes events from the multialorithm GUI
plot_process	plots means during algorithm execution
plot_scatter	makes a scatter plot of data
Predict_performance	predicts the final performance of an algorithm from the learning curve
process_params	receives a parameter vector and returns its components
read_algorithms	reads an algorithm file
start_classify	starts the evaluation of a single classification algorithm
voronoi_regions	makes a Voronoi diagram from 2D sample points

Program descriptions

Below are short descriptions of the programs in the classification toolbox invoked directly by users. This listings are organized by chapter in **Pattern Classification**, and in some cases include pseudo-code. Not all programs here appear in the textbook and not every minor variant on an algorithm in the textbook appears here. While most classification programs take input data sets and targets, some classification and feature selection programs have associated additional inputs and outputs, as listed. You can obtain further specific information on the algorithms by consulting **Pattern Classification** and information on the MATLAB code by using its help command.

Chapter 2

Marginalization Marginalization

Description: This program computes the marginal distribution of a multi-dimensional histogram or distribution as well as the marginal probabilities for test patterns given the "good" features.

Additional inputs: The index of the missing feature and the number of patterns with which to compute the marginal.

Minimum cost classifier `Minimum_cost`

Description: This program performs minimum-cost classification for known distributions and cost matrix λ_{ij}.

Additional input: The cost matrix λ_{ij}.

Normal Density Discriminant Function NDDF

Description: This program computes the mean and d-by-d covariance matrix of each class and then uses them to construct the Bayes decision region.

Additional outputs: The discriminant function (probability) for any test pattern.

Stumps `Stumps`

Description: This program determines the threshold value on a single feature that will yield the lowest training error.

Additional input: The index of the single feature in question.

Additional outputs: The weight vector for the linear classifier arising from the optimal threshold value.

Discrete Bayes Classifier `Discrete_Bayes`

Description: This program performs Bayesian classification on feature vectors having discrete values. In this implementation, discrete features are those that have no more than one decimal place. The program bins the data

Programs for Chapter 2

and then computes the probability of each class. The program then computes the classification decision based on standard Bayes theory.

Multiple Discriminant Analysis `MultipleDiscriminantAnalysis`

Description: This program finds the discriminants for a multi-category problem.

Additional outputs: The weight vectors for the discriminant boundaries.

Bhattacharyya `Bhattacharyya`

Description: This program estimates the Bhattacharyya error rate for a two-category problem.

Chernoff `Chernoff`

Description: This program estimates the Chernoff error rate for a two-category problem.

Discriminability `Discriminability`

Description: This program computes the discriminability d' in the Receiver Operating Characteristic (ROC) curve.

Chapter 3

Maximum-Likelihood Classifier ML

Description: This program computes the maximum-likelihood estimate of the mean and covariance matrix of each class and then uses the results to construct the Bayes decision region.

Maximum-Likelihood Classifier assuming Diagonal Covariance Matrices ML_diag

Description: This program estimates computes the maximum-likelihood estimate of the mean and covariance matrix (assumed diagonal) of each class and then uses the results to construct the Bayes decision region.

Gibbs Gibbs

Description: This program finds the probability that the training data comes from a Gaussian distribution with known parameters, i.e., $P(\mathcal{D}|\theta)$. Then, using $P(\mathcal{D}|\theta)$, the program samples the parameters according to the Gibbs method, and finally uses the parameters to classify the test patterns.

Additional inputs: Resolution of the input features (i.e., the number of bins).

Fishers Linear Discriminant FishersLinearDiscriminant

Description: Computes the Fisher linear discriminant for a pair of distributions.

Additional outputs: The weight vector for the linear classifier.

Programs for Chapter 3

Local Polynomial Classifier `Local_Polynomial`

Description: This nonlinear classification algorithm works by building a classifier based on a local subset of training points, and classifies the test points according to those local classifiers. The method randomly selects a predetermined number of the training points and then assign each of the test points to the nearest of the points so selected. Next, the method builds a logistic classifier around these selected points, and finally classifies the points assigned to it.

Additional inputs: Number of (local) points to select for creation of a local polynomial or logistic classifier.

Expectation-Maximization `Expectation_Maximization`

Description: This program estimates the means and covariances of component Gaussians by the method of expectation-maximization.

Additional inputs: The number of Gaussians for each class.

Additional outputs: The means and covariances of Gaussians.

■ Expectation-Maximization

<u>begin initialize</u> $\theta_0,\ T,\ i \leftarrow 0$

$\quad$ <u>do</u> $\ i \leftarrow i + 1$

$\qquad$ *E step:* compute $\ Q(\theta;\theta^i)$

$\qquad$ *M step:* $\ \theta^{i+1} \leftarrow argmax_\theta Q(\theta;\theta^i)$

$\quad$ <u>until</u> $Q(\theta^{i+1};\theta^i) - Q(\theta^i;\theta^{i-1}) \leq T$

$\quad$ <u>return</u> $\hat{\theta} \leftarrow \theta^{i+1}$

<u>end</u>

Programs for Chapter 3

Multivariate Spline Classification `Multivariate_Splines`

Description: The program fits a spline to the histogram of each of the features of the data. The program then selects the spline that reduces the training error the most, and computes the associated residual of the prediction error. The process iterates on the remaining features, until all have been used. Then, the prediction of each spline is evaluated independently, and the weight of each spline is computed via the pseudo-inverse. This algorithm is typically used for regression but here is used for classification.

Additional inputs: The degree of the splines and the number of knots per spline.

Whitening transform `Whitening_transform`

Description: This program performs a whitening transform on a d-dimensional data set. The program first subtracts the sample mean from each point, and then multiplies the data set by the inverse of the square root of the covariance matrix.

Additional outputs: The whitening matrix and the mean vector.

Scaling transform `Scaling_transform`

Description: This program standardizes the data, that is, transforms a data set so that it has zero mean and unit variance along each coordinate. This scaling is recommended as preprocessing for data presented to a neural network classifier.

Additional outputs: The variance matrix and mean vector.

Programs for Chapter 3

Hidden Markov Model Forward Algorithm HMMForward

Description: This program computes the probability that a test sequence V^T was generated by a given hidden Markov model according to the Forward algorithm.

■ HMM Forward

<u>**begin initialize**</u> $t \leftarrow 0$, a_{ij}, b_{jk}, visible sequence $\mathbf{V}^T$, $\alpha_j(0)$

    <u>**for**</u> $t \leftarrow t + 1$

$$\beta_i(t) \leftarrow \sum_{j=1}^{c} \beta_j(t+1) a_{ij} b_{jk} v(t+1)$$

    <u>**until**</u> t=T

    <u>**return**</u> $P(V^T) \leftarrow \alpha_0(T)$ for the final state

<u>**end**</u>

Hidden Markov Model Backward Algorithm HMMBackward

Description: This program computes the probability that a test sequence V^T was generated by a given hidden Markov model according to the Backward algorithm. Learning in hidden Markov models via the Forward-Backward algorithm makes use of both the Forward and the Backward algorithms.

■ HMM Backward

<u>**begin initialize**</u> $\beta_j(T)$, $t \leftarrow T$, a_{ij}, b_{jk}, visible sequence $\mathbf{V}^T$

    <u>**for**</u> $t \leftarrow t - 1$

Programs for Chapter 3

$$\beta_i(t) \leftarrow \sum_{j=1}^{c} \beta_j(t+1) a_{ij} b_{jk} v(t+1)$$

      until t=1

   return $P(V^T) \leftarrow \beta_i(0)$ for the known initial state

end

Forward-Backward Algorithm `ForwardBackward`

Description: This program estimates the parameters in a hidden Markov model based on a set of training sequences.

■ **Forward-Backward**

begin initialize a_{ij}, b_{jk}, *training sequence* V^T, *convergence criterion* θ, $z \leftarrow 0$

      do $z \leftarrow z + 1$

            compute $\hat{a}(z)$ from $a(z\text{-}1)$ and $b(z\text{-}1)$

            compute $\hat{b}(z)$ from $a(z\text{-}1)$ and $b(z\text{-}1)$

            $a_{ij}(z) \leftarrow \hat{a}_{ij}(z-1)$

            $b_{jk}(z) \leftarrow \hat{b}_{jk}(z-1)$

      until $max_{i,j,k}\left[a_{ij}(z)-a_{ij}(z-1), b_{jk}(z) - b_{jk}(z-1)\right] < \theta$

   return $a_{ij} \leftarrow a_{ij}(z)$, $b_{jk} \leftarrow b_{jk}(z)$

end

Programs for Chapter 3

Hidden Markov Model Decoding HMMDecoding

Description: This algorithm estimates a highly likely path through the hidden Markov model (trellis) based on the topology and transition probabilities in that model.

■ **HMM Decoding**

<u>begin initialize</u> $Path \leftarrow \{...\}$, $t \leftarrow 0$

$\qquad$ <u>for</u> $t \leftarrow t + 1$

$\qquad$ $j \leftarrow j + 1$

$\qquad$ <u>for</u> $j \leftarrow j + 1$

$$\alpha_j(t) \leftarrow b_{jk}v(t)\sum_{i=1}^{c}\alpha_i(t-1)a_{ij}$$

$\qquad$ <u>until</u> $j = c$

$\qquad$ $j' \leftarrow \arg max_j \alpha_j(t)$

$\qquad$ *Append* $\omega_{j'}$ *to Path*

$\qquad$ <u>until</u> $t = T$

$\qquad$ <u>*return*</u> *Path*

<u>end</u>

Chapter 4

Nearest-Neighbor Classifier `Nearest_Neighbor`

Description: For each of the test examples, the nearest k neighbors from training examples are found, and the majority label among these are given as the label to the test example.

Additional inputs: Number of nearest neighbors, k.

Nearest-Neighbor Editing `NearestNeighborEditing`

Description: This algorithm searches for the Voronoi neighbors of each pattern. If the labels of all the neighbors are the same, the pattern in discarded. The MATLAB implementation uses linear programming to increase speed.

■ **Nearest-Neighbor Editing**

<u>begin initialize</u> $j \leftarrow 0$, $\mathcal{D} \leftarrow data\ set$, $n \leftarrow num\ prototypes$

        construct the full Voronoid diagram of $\mathcal{D}$

        <u>do</u> $j \leftarrow j + 1$; for each prototype x_j'

            find the Voronoi neighbors of x_j'

            <u>if</u> any neighbor is not from the same class as x_j' <u>then</u> mark x_j'

      <u>until</u> $j = n$

      discard all points that are not marked

      construct the Voronoi diagram of the remaining (marked) prototypes

<u>end</u>

Programs for Chapter 4

Store-Grabbag Algorithm `Store_Grabbag`

Description: The store-grabbag algorithm is a modification of the nearest-neighbor algorithm. The program identifies those samples in the training set that affect the classification, and discards the others.

Additional inputs: Number of nearest neighbors, k.

Reduced Coloumb Energy `RCE`

Description: This program creates a classifier based on a training set, maximizing the radius around each training point (up to λ_{max}) yet not misclassifying other training points.

Additional inputs: The maximum allowable radius, λ_{max}.

■ RCE Training

<u>**begin initialize**</u> $j \leftarrow 0$, $n \leftarrow num\ patterns$, $\varepsilon \leftarrow small\ param$, $\lambda_m \leftarrow max\ radius$

$\quad\quad$ <u>**do**</u> $j \leftarrow j + 1$

$\quad\quad\quad\quad w_{ij} \leftarrow x_i$ (train weight)

$\quad\quad\quad\quad \hat{x} \leftarrow \arg min_{x \notin \omega_i} D(x, x')$ (find nearest point not in ω_i)

$\quad\quad\quad\quad \lambda_j \leftarrow min\left[D(\hat{x}, x') - \varepsilon, \lambda_m\right]$ (set radius)

$\quad\quad$ <u>**if**</u> $x \in \omega_k$ <u>**then**</u> $a_{jk} \leftarrow 1$

$\quad$ <u>**until**</u> $j = n$

<u>**end**</u>

■ RCE Classification

<u>**begin initialize**</u> $j \leftarrow 0$, $k \leftarrow 0$, $x \leftarrow test\ pattern$, $\mathcal{D}_t \leftarrow \{\dots\}$

        <u>**do**</u> $j \leftarrow j + 1$

                <u>**if**</u> $D(x, x_j') < \lambda_j$ <u>**then**</u> $\mathcal{D}_t \leftarrow \mathcal{D}_t \cup x_j'$

        <u>**until**</u> $j = n$

        <u>**if**</u> label of all $x_j' \in \mathcal{D}_t$ is the same <u>**then return**</u> label of all $x_k \in \mathcal{D}_t$

                                <u>**else return**</u> "ambiguous" label

<u>**end**</u>

Parzen Windows Classifier `Parzen`

Description: This program estimates a posterior density by convolving the data set in each category with a Gaussian Parzen window of scale h.

Additional inputs: Normalizing factor for the window width, h.

Probabilistic Neural Network Classification PNN

Description: This algorithm estimates a posterior density by convolving the data set in each category with a Gaussian Parzen window of scale h.

Additional inputs: Normalizing factor for the window width, h.

Programs for Chapter 4

■ PNN Classification

<u>**begin initialize**</u> $k \leftarrow 0$, $x \leftarrow test\ pattern$

        <u>**do**</u> $k \leftarrow k + 1$

            $net_k \leftarrow w_k^t x$

            <u>**if**</u> $a_{ki} = 1$ <u>**then**</u> $g_i \leftarrow g_i + \exp[(net_k - 1)/\sigma^2]$

      <u>**return**</u> $class \leftarrow argmax_i\ g_i(x)$

<u>**end**</u>

Chapter 5

Basic Gradient Descent `BasicGradientDescent`

Description: This program performs simple gradient descent in a scalar-valued criterion function $J(a)$.

■ Basic Gradient Descent

<u>**begin initialize**</u> a, threshold θ, $\eta(.)$, $k \leftarrow 0$

        <u>**do**</u> $k \leftarrow k + 1$

            $a \leftarrow a - \eta(k)\nabla J(a)$

        <u>**until**</u> $|\eta(k)\nabla J(a)| < \theta$

      <u>**return**</u> a

<u>**end**</u>

Programs for Chapter 5

Newton Gradient Descent `Newton_descent`

Description: This program performs Newton's method for gradient descent in a scalar-valued criterion function $J(a)$, where the Hessian matrix is H.

■ Newton Descent

<u>begin initialize</u> a, threshold θ

        <u>do</u>

$$a \leftarrow a - H^{-1}\nabla J(a)$$

        <u>until</u> $|H^{-1}\nabla J(a)| < \theta$

     <u>return</u> a

<u>end</u>

Batch Perceptron `Perceptron_Batch`

Description: This program trains a linear Perceptron classifier in batch mode.

Additional inputs: The maximum number of iterations, the convergence criterion and the convergence rate.

Additional outputs: The weight vector for the linear classifier and the weights throughout learning.

■ Batch Perceptron

<u>begin initialize</u> a, criterion θ, $\eta(.)$, $k \leftarrow 0$

        <u>do</u> $k \leftarrow k + 1$

$$a \leftarrow a + \eta(k) \sum_{y \in \mathcal{Y}_k} y$$

Programs for Chapter 5

$$\text{\underline{until}} \left| \eta(k) \sum_{y \in \mathcal{Y}_k} y \right| < \theta$$

> > **return** *a*

end

Fixed-Increment Single-Sample Perceptron `Perceptron_FIS`

Description: This program attempts to iteratively find a linear separating hyperplane. If the problem is linear, the algorithm is guaranteed to find a solution. During the iterative learning process the algorithm randomly selects a sample from the training set and tests if that sample is correctly classified. If not, the weight vector of the classifier is updated. The algorithm iterates until all training samples are correctly classified or the maximal number of training iterations is reached.

Addition inputs: The parameters describing either the maximum number of iterations, or a weight vector for the training samples, or both.

Additional outputs: The weight vector for the linear classifier.

■ Fixed-Increment Single-Sample Perceptron

begin initialize *a*, $k \leftarrow 0$

> **do** $k \leftarrow (k + 1) \bmod n$

> > **if** $\mathbf{y}^k$ is misclassified by **a then** $a \leftarrow a + y^k$

> > **until** all patterns properly classified

> **return a**

end

Variable-increment Perceptron with Margin `Perceptron_VIM`

Description: This program trains a linear Perceptron classifier with a margin by adjusting the weight step size.

Additional inputs: The margin b, the maximum number of iterations, the convergence criterion and the convergence rate.

Additional outputs: The weight vector for the linear classifier.

■ Variable-increment Perceptron with Margin

<u>**begin initialize**</u> a, threshold θ, margin b, $\eta(.)$, $k \leftarrow 0$

    <u>**do**</u> $k \leftarrow (k + 1) mod\ n$

        <u>**if**</u> $a^t y^k \leq b$ <u>**then**</u> $a \leftarrow a + \eta(k)y^k$

        <u>**until**</u> $a^t y^k > b$ for all k

    <u>**return a**</u>

<u>**end**</u>

Batch Variable Increment Perceptron `Perceptron_BVI`

Description: This algorithm trains a linear Perceptron classifier in the batch mode, and where the learning rate is variable.

■ Batch Variable Increment Perceptron

<u>**begin initialize**</u> a, $\eta(.)$, $k \leftarrow 0$

    <u>**do**</u> $k \leftarrow (k + 1) mod\ n$

Programs for Chapter 5

$$\mathcal{Y}_k = \{\}$$

$$j = 0$$

do $j \leftarrow j + 1$

       if $\mathbf{y}_j$ is misclassified **then** Append $\mathbf{y}_j$ is to $\mathcal{Y}_k$

    until $j = n$

$$a \leftarrow a + \eta(k) \sum_{y \in \mathcal{Y}_k} y$$

    until $\mathcal{Y}_k = \{\}$

   return a

end

Balanced Winnow `Balanced_Winnow`

Description: This program implements the balanced Winnow algorithm, which uses both a positive and negative weight vectors, each adjusted toward the final decision boundary from opposite sides.

Additional inputs: The maximum number of iterations, the scaling parameter, and the convergence rate.

Additional outputs: The positive weight vector and the negative weight vector.

■ **Balanced Winnow**

begin initialize $\mathbf{a}^+$, $\mathbf{a}^-$, $\eta(.)$, $k \leftarrow 0$, $\alpha > 1$

    if $\text{Sgn}[\mathbf{a}^{+t}\mathbf{y}_k - \mathbf{a}^{-t}\mathbf{y}_k] \neq z_k$ (pattern misclassified)

    then if $z_k = +1$ **then** $a_i^\dagger \leftarrow \alpha^{y_i} a_i^\dagger$; $a_i^- \leftarrow \alpha^{-y_i} a_i^-$ for all i

       if $z_k = -1$ **then** $a_i^\dagger \leftarrow \alpha^{-y_i} a_i^\dagger$; $a_i^- \leftarrow \alpha^{y_i} a_i^-$ for all i

<u>**return a⁺, a⁻**</u>

<u>**end**</u>

Batch Relaxation with Margin `Relaxation_BM`

Description: This program trains a linear Perceptron classifier with margin b in the batch mode.

Additional inputs: The maximum number of iterations, the target margin b, and the convergence rate.

Additional outputs: The weight vector for the final linear classifier.

■ Batch Relaxation with Margin

<u>**begin initialize**</u> a, $\eta(.)$, b, $k \leftarrow 0$

  <u>**do**</u> $k \leftarrow (k + 1) \bmod n$

    $\mathcal{Y}_k = \{\}$

    $j = 0$

    <u>**do**</u> $j \leftarrow j + 1$

       <u>**if**</u> $a^t y^j \leq b$ <u>**then**</u> Append y_j is to $\mathcal{Y}_k$

    <u>**until**</u> $j = n$

    $a \leftarrow a + \eta(k) \displaystyle\sum_{y \in \mathcal{Y}_k} \frac{b - a^t y}{|y|^2}$

    <u>**until**</u> $\mathcal{Y}_k = \{\}$

  <u>**return a**</u>

<u>**end**</u>

Programs for Chapter 5

Single-Sample Relaxation with Margin `Relaxation_SSM`

Description: This program trains a linear Perceptron classifier with margin on a per-pattern basis.

Additional inputs: The maximum number of iterations, the margin b, and the convergence rate.

Additional outputs: The weight vector for the final linear classifier.

■ **Single-Sample Relaxation with Margin**

<u>begin initialize</u> a, b, $\eta(.)$, $k \leftarrow 0$

$\qquad$ <u>do</u> $k \leftarrow (k+1) \bmod n$

$$\underline{\text{if}} \ a^t y^j \le b \ \underline{\text{then}} \ a \leftarrow a + \eta(k)\frac{b - a^t y^k}{\left|y^k\right|^2} y^k$$

$\qquad\qquad$ <u>until</u> $a^t y^k > b$ for all y^k

$\qquad$ <u>return a</u>

<u>end</u>

Least-Mean Square LMS

Description: This program trains a linear Perceptron classifier using the least-mean square algorithm.

Additional inputs: The maximum number of iterations, the convergence criterion, and the convergence rate.

Additional outputs: The final weight vector and the weight vector throughout the training procedure.

■ LMS

begin initialize a, b, threshold θ, $\eta(.)$, $k \leftarrow 0$

        do $k \leftarrow (k+1) mod\ n$

                $a \leftarrow a + \eta(k)(b_k - a^t y^k)y^k$

                until $\left| \eta(k)(b_k - a^t y^k) \right| < \theta$

        return a

end

Least-Squares Classifier LS

Description: This algorithm trains a linear Perceptron classifier by computing the weight vector using the Moore-Penrose pseudo-inverse.

Additional inputs: An optional weight vector for *weighted* least squares.

Additional outputs: The weight vector of the final trained classifier.

Ho-Kashyap Ho_Kashyap

Description: This program trains a linear classifier by the Ho-Kashyap algorithm.

Additional inputs: The type of training (Basic or modified), the maximum number of iterations, the convergence criterion, and the convergence rate.

Additional outputs: The weights for the linear classifier and the final computed margin.

Programs for Chapter 5

■ **Ho-Kashyap**

<u>**begin initialize**</u> a, b, $\eta(.) < 1$, threshold b_{min}, k_{max}

      <u>**do**</u> $k \leftarrow (k+1) \bmod n$

            $e \leftarrow Ya - b$

            $e^{\dagger} \leftarrow 1/2(e + Abs(e))$

            $b \leftarrow b + 2\eta(k)e^{\dagger}$

            $a \leftarrow Y^{\dagger}b$

            <u>**if**</u> $Abs(e) \leq b_{min}$ <u>**then**</u> <u>**return**</u> a, b and <u>**exit**</u>

      <u>**until**</u> $k = k_{max}$

Print "NO SOLUTION FOUND"

<u>**end**</u>

■ **Modified Ho-Kashyap**

<u>**begin initialize**</u> a, b, $\eta < 1$, threshold b_{min}, k_{max}

      <u>**do**</u> $k \leftarrow (k+1) \bmod n$

            $e \leftarrow Ya - b$

            $e^{\dagger} \leftarrow 1/2(e + Abs(e))$

            $b \leftarrow b + 2\eta(k)(e + Abs(e))$

            $a \leftarrow Y^{\dagger}b$

            <u>**if**</u> $Abs(e) \leq b_{min}$ <u>**then**</u> <u>**return**</u> a, b and <u>**exit**</u>

      <u>**until**</u> $k = k_{max}$

Print "NO SOLUTION FOUND"

<u>**end**</u>

Voted Perceptron Classifier `Perceptron_Voted`

Description: The voted Perceptron is a variant of the Perceptron where, in this implementation, the data may be transformed using a kernel function so as to increase the separation between classes.

Pocket Algorithm `Pocket`

Description: The pocket algorithm is a simple modification over the Perceptron algorithm. The improvement is that updates to the weight vector are retained only if they perform better on a random sample of the data. In the current MATLAB implementation, the weight vector is trained for 10 iterations. Then, the new weight vector and the previous weight vector are used to train randomly selected training patterns. If the new weight vector succeeded in classifying more patterns before it misclassified a pattern compared to the old weight vector, the new weight vector replaces the old weight vector. The procedure is repeated until convergence or the maximum number of iterations is reached.

Additional inputs: Either the maximal number of iterations or weight vector for the training samples, or both.

Additional outputs: The weight vector for the final linear classifier.

Farthest-margin perceptron `Perceptron_FM`

Description: This program implements a slight variation on the traditional Perceptron algorithm, with the only difference that the wrongly classified sample *farthest* from the current decision boundary is used to adjust the weight of the classifier.

Additional inputs: The maximum number of iterations and the slack for incorrectly classified examples

Additional outputs: The weight vector for the trained linear classifier.

Programs for Chapter 5

Support Vector Machine SVM

Description: This program implements a support vector machine and works in two stages. In the first stage, the program transforms the data by a kernel function; in the second stage, the program finds a linear separating hyperplane. The first stage depends on the selected kernel function and the second stage depends on the algorithmic `solver` method selected by the user. The solver can be a quadratic programming algorithm, a simple farthest-margin Perceptron, or the Lagrangian algorithm. The number of support vectors found will usually be larger than is actually needed if the first two solvers are used because both solvers are approximate.

Additional inputs: The kernel function: `Gauss` (or `RBF`), `Poly`, `Sigmoid`, or `Linear`. For each kernel parameters the following parameters are needed:

- RBF kernel: Gaussian width (scalar parameter)
- Poly kernel: The integer degree of the polynomial
- Sigmoid: The slope and constant of the sigmoid
- Linear: no parameters are needed

Another additional input is the choice of solver: `Perceptron`, `Quadprog`, or `Lagrangian`.

The final input parameter is the slack, or tolerance.

Additional outputs: The SVM coefficients.

Regularized Descriminant Analysis RDA

Description: This program functions much as does the ML algorithm. However, once the mean and covariance of Gaussians are estimated they are shrunk.

Additional input: The shrinkage coefficient.

Chapter 6

Stochastic Backpropagation `Backpropagation_Stochastic`

Description: This program implements the stochastic backpropagation learning algorithm in a three-layer network of nonlinear units.

Additional inputs: The number of hidden units n_H, the convergence criterion θ, and the convergence rate.

Additional outputs: The input-to-hidden weights w_{ji}, the hidden-to-output weights w_{kj}, and the training and test errors through the training.

■ Stochastic Backpropagation

<u>**begin initialize**</u> n_H, w, criterion θ, η, $m \leftarrow 0$

      <u>**do**</u> $m \leftarrow m + 1$

            $x^m \leftarrow randomly\ chosen\ pattern$

            $w_{ji} \leftarrow w_{ji} + \eta \delta_j x_i$; $w_{kj} \leftarrow w_{kj} + \eta \delta_k y_j$

      <u>**until**</u> $\|\nabla J(w)\| < \theta$

   <u>**return**</u> w

<u>**end**</u>

■ Stochastic Backpropagation with Momentum

<u>**begin initialize**</u> n_H, w, $\alpha(<1)$, θ, η, $m \leftarrow 0$, $b_{ji} \leftarrow 0$, $b_{kj} \leftarrow 0$

      <u>**do**</u> $m \leftarrow m + 1$

          $x^m \leftarrow randomly\ chosen\ pattern$

          $b_{ji} \leftarrow \eta(1 - \alpha)\delta_j x_i + \alpha b_{ji}$; $b_{kj} \leftarrow \eta(1 - \alpha)\delta_k y_j + \alpha b_{kj}$

Programs for Chapter 6

$$\underline{\textbf{until}} \ \|\nabla J(w)\| < \theta$$

$$\underline{\textbf{return}} \ w$$

$\underline{\textbf{end}}$

Batch Backpropagation `Backpropagation_Batch`

Description: This program implements the batch backpropagation learning algorithm in a three-layer network of nonlinear units.

Additional inputs: The number of hidden units n_H, the convergence criterion θ, and the convergence rate.

Additional outputs: The input-to-hidden weights w_{ji}, the hidden-to-output weights w_{kj}, and the training and test errors through the training.

■ Batch Backpropagation

$\underline{\textbf{begin initialize}} \ n_H, w, \text{criterion } \theta, \eta, \ r \leftarrow 0$

$\qquad \underline{\textbf{do}} \ \ r \leftarrow r + 1 \quad (\text{increment epoch})$

$\qquad\qquad m \leftarrow 0; \ \Delta w_{ji} \leftarrow 0; \ \Delta w_{kj} \leftarrow 0$

$\qquad\qquad \underline{\textbf{do}} \ m \leftarrow m + 1$

$\qquad\qquad\qquad x^m \leftarrow select \ pattern$

$\qquad\qquad\qquad \Delta w_{ji} \leftarrow \Delta w_{ji} + \eta \delta_j x_i \ ; \Delta w_{kj} \leftarrow \Delta w_{kj} + \eta \delta_k y_j$

$\qquad\qquad \underline{\textbf{until}} \ m = n$

$\qquad\qquad w_{ji} \leftarrow w_{ji} + \eta \delta_j x_i; \ w_{kj} \leftarrow w_{kj} + \eta \delta_k y_j$

$\qquad \underline{\textbf{until}} \ \|\nabla J(w)\| < \theta$

$\qquad\qquad \underline{\textbf{return}} \ w$

$\underline{\textbf{end}}$

Programs for Chapter 6

Backpropagation trained using Conjugate Gradient Descent Backpropagation_CGD

Description: This program trains a three-layer network of nonlinear units using conjugate gradient descent.

Additional inputs: The number of hidden units, n_H, and the convergence criterion θ.

Additional outputs: The input-to-hidden weights w_{ji}, the hidden-to-output weights w_{kj}, and the training and test errors through the training.

Recurrent Backpropagation Backpropagation_Recurrent

Description: This program trains a three-layer network of nonlinear units having recurrent connections. The network is fed with the inputs, and these are propagated until the network stabilizes. Then the weights are changed just as in traditional feed-forward networks.

Additional inputs: The number of hidden units n_H, the convergence criterion θ, and convergence rate.

Additional outputs: The connection weights and the errors through the training.

Cascade-Correlation Cascade_Correlation

Description: This program trains a nonlinear cascade-correlation network.

Additional inputs: The converge criterion and the convergence rate.

Additional outputs: Input-to-hidden weights, hidden-to-output weights and the errors throughout training.

Programs for Chapter 6

■ Cascade-Correlation

<u>**begin initialize**</u> a, criterion θ, η, $k \leftarrow 0$

    <u>**do**</u> $m \leftarrow m + 1$

        $w_{ki} \leftarrow w_{ki} - \eta \nabla J(w)$

    <u>**until**</u> $\|\nabla J(w)\| < \theta$

    <u>**if**</u> $J(w) > \theta$ <u>**then**</u> add hidden unit <u>**until**</u> <u>**exit**</u>

        <u>**do**</u> $m \leftarrow m + 1$

        $w_{ji} \leftarrow w_{ji} - \eta \nabla J(w)$; $w_{kj} \leftarrow w_{kj} - \eta \nabla J(w)$

    <u>**until**</u> $\|\nabla J(w)\| < \theta$

    <u>**return**</u> w

<u>**end**</u>

Optimal Brain Surgeon `Optimal_Brain_Surgeon`

Description: This program prunes a trained three-layer network by means of Optimal Brain Surgeon or Optimal Brain Damage.

Additional inputs: The initial number of hidden units and the convergence (error) criterion.

Additional outputs: The input-to-hidden weights, the hidden-to-output weights, and the errors throughout training.

■ Optimal Brain Surgeon

<u>**begin initialize**</u> n_H, a, θ

    train a reasonably large network to minimum error

    <u>**do**</u> compute H^{-1} (inverse Hessian matrix)

$$q^* \leftarrow \arg\min_q \frac{w_q^2}{2[H^{-1}]_{qq}} \quad (\text{saliency } L_q)$$

$$w \leftarrow w - \frac{w_{q^*}}{[H^{-1}]_{q^*q^*}} H^{-1} e_{q^*}$$

<u>until</u> $J(w) > \theta$

<u>return</u> w

<u>end</u>

Quickprop `Backpropagation_Quickprop`

Description: This program trains a three-layer network by means of the Quickprop algorithm.

Additional inputs: The number of hidden units n_H, the convergence criterion, the convergence rate, and the error correction rate.

Additional outputs: The input-to-hidden weights, the hidden-to-output weights, and the errors through the training.

Projection Pursuit `Projection_Pursuit`

Description: This program implements the projection pursuit statistical estimation procedure.

Additional inputs: The number of component features onto which the data is projected.

Additional outputs: The component weights and the output unit weights

Programs for Chapter 6

Radial Basis Function Classifier `RBF_Network`

Description: This program trains a radial basis function classifier. First the program computes the centers for the data using k-means. Then the algorithm estimates the variance of the data around each center, and uses this estimate to compute the activation of each training pattern to these centers. These activation patterns are used for computing the gating unit of the classifier, via the Moore-Penrose pseudo-inverse.

Additional inputs: The number of hidden units.

Additional outputs: The locations in feature space of the centers of the hidden units, and the weights of the gating units.

Chapter 7

Stochastic Simulated Annealing `Stochastic_SA`

Description: This program performs stochastic simulated annealing in a network of binary units.

Additional inputs: The number of output data points and the cooling rate.

■ Stochastic Simulated Annealing

<u>**begin initialize**</u> $T(k)$, k_{max}, $s_i(1)$, w_{ij} for $i, j = 1, \dots N$

$\qquad k \leftarrow 0$

$\qquad\qquad$ <u>**do**</u> $k \leftarrow k + 1$

$\qquad\qquad\qquad$ <u>**do**</u> select node i randomly; suppose its state is s_i

$$E_a \leftarrow -1/2 \sum_{j}^{\mathfrak{N}_i} w_{ij} s_i s_j$$

$$E_b \leftarrow -E_a$$

$$\underline{\textbf{if}}\ E_b < E_a$$

$$\underline{\textbf{then}}\ s_i \leftarrow -s_i$$

$$\underline{\textbf{else}}\ \underline{\textbf{if}}\ e^{-\dfrac{(E_b - E_a)}{T(k)}} > Rand[0, 1]$$

$$\underline{\textbf{then}}\ s_i \leftarrow -s_i$$

$$\underline{\textbf{until}}\ \text{all nodes polled several times}$$

$$\underline{\textbf{until}}\ k = k_{max}\ \text{or stopping criterion met}$$

$$\underline{\textbf{return}}\ E,\ s_i,\ \text{for}\ i = 1, \dots N$$

$\underline{\textbf{end}}$

Deterministic Simulated Annealing `Deterministic_SA`

Description: This program performs deterministic simulated annealing in a network of binary units.

Additional inputs: The number of clusters and the cooling rate.

■ Deterministic Simulated Annealing

$\underline{\textbf{begin initialize}}\ T(k),\ w_{ij},\ s_i(1)\ \text{for}\ i, j = 1, \dots N$

$$k \leftarrow 0$$

$$\underline{\textbf{do}}\ k \leftarrow k + 1$$

$$\text{select node } i \text{ randomly}$$

$$l_i \leftarrow \sum_{j}^{\mathfrak{N}_i} w_{ij} s_j$$

$$s_i \leftarrow f(l_i, T(k))$$

Programs for Chapter 7

$\underline{\textbf{until}}$ $k = k_{max}$ or stopping criterion met

$\underline{\textbf{return}}$ E, s_i, for $i = 1, \ldots N$

$\underline{\textbf{end}}$

Deterministic Boltzmann Learning `BoltzmannLearning`

Description: In this implementation, we train weak learners, and find the best combination of these classifiers.

Additional inputs: The number of input units, the number of hidden units, the ooling rate, the type of weak learner and their parameters.

Additional outputs: The errors during training.

■ Deterministic Boltzmann Learning

$\underline{\textbf{begin initialize}}$ $\mathcal{D}$, η, $T(k)$, w_{ij} for $i, j = 1, \ldots N$

$\qquad \underline{\textbf{do}}$ randomly select training pattern x

$\qquad\qquad$ randomize states s_i

$\qquad\qquad$ anneal network with input and output clamped

$\qquad\qquad$ at final, low T, calculate $[s_i s_j]_{\alpha^i \alpha^o clamped}$

$\qquad\qquad$ randomize states s_i

$\qquad\qquad$ anneal network with input clamped but output free

$\qquad\qquad$ at final, low T, calculate $[s_i s_j]_{\alpha^i clamped}$

$\qquad\qquad w_{ij} \leftarrow w_{ij} + (\eta / T)[[s_i s_j]_{\alpha^i \alpha^o clamped} - [s_i s_j]_{\alpha^i clamped}]$

$\qquad\qquad \underline{\textbf{until}}$ $k = k_{max}$ or stopping criterion met

$\qquad \underline{\textbf{return}}$ w_{ij}

$\underline{\textbf{end}}$

Programs for Chapter 7

Basic Genetic Algorithm `Genetic_Algorithm`

Description: This program uses a basic genetic algorithm to build a classifier from component weak classifiers.

Additional inputs: The probability of cross-over P_{co}, the probability of mutation P_{mut}, the type of weak classifier and their parameters, the target or stopping error on training set, and the number of solutions to be returned by the program.

■ Basic Genetic Algorithm

begin initialize θ, P_{co}, P_{mut}, L N-bit chromosomes

        do determine the fitness of each chromosome f_i, $i = 1,..., L$

            rank the chromosomes

            do select two chromosomes with the highest score

                if Rand[0,1) $< P_{co}$ **then** crossover the pair at a randommly chosen bit

                        else change each bit with proability P_{mut};

                            remove the parent chromosomes

            until N offspring have been created

        until any chromosome's score f exceeds θ

      return highest fitness chromosome (best classifier)

end

Genetic Programming `Genetic_Programming`

Description: This program approximates a function by evolving mathematical expressions by a genetic programming algorithm.

Additional inputs: The initial function length, the number of generations, and the number of solutions to be returned by the program.

Programs for Chapter 7

Chapter 8

C4.5 `c4.5`

Description: The program constructs a decision tree recursively so as to minimize the error on a training set. Discrete features are split using a histogram and continuous features are split using an information criteria. The program is implemented under the assumption that a pattern vector with fewer than 10 unique values is discrete, and will be treated as such. Other vectors are treated as continuous. Note that due to MATLAB memoery and processing restrictions, the recursion depth may be reached during the processing of a large complicated data set, which will result in an error.

Additional inputs: The maximum percentage of error at a node that will prevent it from further splitting.

ID3 `ID3`

Description: The program constructs a decision tree recursively so as to minimize the error on a training set. The criterion for splitting a node is either the percentage of incorrectly classified samples at the node, or the entropy at the node, or the variance of the outputs. Note that due to MATLAB memoery and processing restrictions, the recursion depth may be reached during the processing of a large complicated data set, which will result in an error.

Additional inputs: The splitting criterion (`entropy`, `variance`, or `misclassification`)

Naive String Matching `Naive_String_Matching`

Description: This program performs naive string matching, which is quite inefficient in the general case. The value of this program is primarily for making performance comparisons with the Boyer-Moore algorithm.

Programs for Chapter 8

■ **Naive String Matching**

begin initialize @, *a*, *n* ← length[*text*], *m* ← length[*x*]

    s ← 0

        while *s* < *n* - *m*

                if **x**[*1...m*] = *text*[*s+1...s+m*]

                        then *print* "pattern occurs at shift" *s*

                           s ← *s* + 1

    return

end

Boyer-Moor String Matching `Boyer_Moore_string_matching`

Description: This program performs string matching by the Boyer-Moore algorithm, which is typically far more efficient than naive string matching.

■ **Boyer-Moore String Matching**

begin initialize @, *a*, *n* ← length[*text*], *m* ← length[*x*]

    $\mathcal{F}(x)$ ← last -occurence function

    $\mathcal{Z}(x)$ ← good-suffix function

        s ← 0

        while *s* ≤ *n* - *m*

                do *j* ← *m*

                while *j* > *0* and **x**[*j*] = *text*[*s+j*]

                        do *j* ← *j* – 1

                        if *j* = *0*

Programs for Chapter 8

$$\textbf{then } print \text{ "pattern occurs at shift" } s$$

$$s \leftarrow s + \mathcal{G}(0)$$

$$\textbf{else } s \leftarrow s + \max[\mathcal{G}(j), j - \mathcal{F}(text[s + j])]$$

   return

end

Edit Distance `Edit_Distance`

Description: This program computes the edit distance between two strings x and y.

■ **Edit Distance**

begin initialize $\mathcal{Q}, x, y, \quad m \leftarrow \text{length}[x], \quad n \leftarrow \text{length}[y]$

   $C[0, 0] \leftarrow 0$

   $i \leftarrow 0$

   do $i \leftarrow i + 1$

        $C[i, 0] \leftarrow i$

   until $i = m$

   $j \leftarrow 0$

   do $j \leftarrow j + 1$

        $C[0, j] \leftarrow j$

   until $j = n$

   $i \leftarrow 0; j \leftarrow 0$

   do $i \leftarrow i + 1$

        do $j \leftarrow j + 1$

            $C[i,j] = \min[C[i\text{-}1,j] + 1, C[i,j\text{-}1]+1, C[i\text{-}1,j\text{-}1]+ 1 - \delta(x[i],y[j])]$

$$\underline{\textbf{until}} \; j = n$$
$$\underline{\textbf{until}} \; i = m$$
$$\underline{\textbf{return}} \; \mathbf{C}[m,n]$$
end

Bottom-Up Parsing Bottom_Up_Parsing

Description: This program perfoms bottom-up parsing of a string x in grammar G.

■ **Bottom-Up Parsing**

$\underline{\textbf{begin initialize}} \; G = (\mathcal{Q}, \mathcal{G}, \mathcal{S}, \mathcal{P}), \; \mathbf{x} = x_1 x_2 ... x_n$

    $i \leftarrow 0$

    $\underline{\textbf{do}} \; i \leftarrow i + 1$

        $V_{i1} \leftarrow \{A | A \rightarrow x_i\}$

    $\underline{\textbf{until}} \; i = n$

    $j \leftarrow 1$

    $\underline{\textbf{do}} \; j \leftarrow j + 1$

        $i \leftarrow 0$

        $\underline{\textbf{do}} \; i \leftarrow i + 1$

            $V_{ij} \leftarrow \varnothing$

            $k \leftarrow 0$

            $\underline{\textbf{do}} \; k \leftarrow k + 1$

                $V_{ij} \leftarrow V_{ij} \cup \{A | A \rightarrow BC \in P, B \in V_{ik} \text{and} C \in V_{i+k, j-k}\}$

            $\underline{\textbf{until}} \; k = j - 1$

        $\underline{\textbf{until}} \; i = n - j + 1$

Programs for Chapter 8

$\qquad$ **until** $j = n$

$\qquad$ **if** $S \in V_{1n}$ **then** *print* "parse of" x "successful in G"

$\quad$ **return**

end

Grammatical Inference (Overview) `Grammatical_Inference`

Description: This program infers a grammar G from a set of positive and negative example strings and a (simple) initial grammar G^0.

■ **Grammatical Inference (Overview)**

begin initialize $\mathcal{D}^+, \mathcal{D}^-, G^0$

$\qquad n^\dagger \leftarrow |D^\dagger|$ (number of instances in $\mathcal{D}^+$)

$\qquad\quad \mathcal{S} \leftarrow S$

$\qquad\quad \mathcal{Q} \leftarrow$ set of characters in $\mathcal{D}^+$

$\qquad\quad i \leftarrow 0$

$\qquad\quad$ **do** $i \leftarrow i + 1$

$\qquad\qquad\qquad$ read x_i^+ from $\mathcal{D}^+$

$\qquad\qquad\qquad$ **if** x_i^+ cannot be parsed by G

$\qquad\qquad\qquad$ **then do** propose additional productions to $\mathcal{P}$ and variables to $\mathcal{S}$

$\qquad\qquad\qquad\qquad$ accept updates if G parses x_i^+ but no string in $\mathcal{D}^-$

$\qquad\qquad\qquad$ **until** $i = n^+$

$\qquad\qquad\qquad$ eliminate redundant productions

$\qquad$ **return** $G \leftarrow \{\mathcal{Q}, \mathcal{S}, \mathcal{S}, \mathcal{P}\}$

end

Chapter 9

AdaBoost `Ada_Boost`

Description: AdaBoost builds a nonlinear classifier by constructing an ensemble of "weak" classifiers (i.e., ones that need perform only slightly better than chance) so that the joint decision is has better accuracy on the training set. It is possible to iteratively add classifiers so as to attain any given accuracy on the training set. In AdaBoost each sample of the training set is selected for training the weak with a probability proportional to how well it is classified. An incorrectly classified sample will be chosen more frequently for the training, and will thus be more likely to be correctly classified by the new weak classifier.

Additional inputs: The input parameters are the number of boosting iterations, the name of weak learner and its parameters.

Additional outputs: The training errors throughout the learning.

■ **AdaBoost**

<u>**begin initialize**</u> $\mathcal{D} = \{x^1, y_1, \dots x^n, y_n\}$, k_{max}, $W_1(i) = 1/n$, $i = 1, \dots, n$

    $k \leftarrow 0$

    <u>**do**</u> $k \leftarrow k + 1$

        train weak learner C_k using $\mathcal{D}$ sampled according to $W_k(i)$

        $E_k \leftarrow$ training error of C_k measured on $\mathcal{D}$ using $W_k(i)$

        $\alpha_k \leftarrow \frac{1}{2} \ln[(1 - E_k)/E_k]$

$$W_{k+1}(i) \leftarrow \frac{W_k(i)}{Z_k} \times \begin{cases} e^{-\alpha_k} \, if \, h_k(x^i) = y_i \\ e^{\alpha_k} \, if \, h_k(x^i) \neq y_i \end{cases}$$

        <u>**until**</u> $k = k_{max}$

Programs for Chapter 9

$\qquad$ **return** C_k and α_k for $k = 1$ to k_{max} (ensemble of classifiers with weights)

end

Local boosting `LocBoost`

Description: This program creates a single nonlinear classifier based on boosting of localized classifiers. The algorithm assigns local classifiers to incorrectly classified training data, and optimizes these local classifiers to reach the minimum error.

Additional inputs: The number of boosting iterations, the number of EM iterations, the number of optimization steps, the type of weak learner and its parameters.

Additional outputs: Posterior probabilities for the training points, the parameters of the weak classifiers and the parameters of the gating functions that weight the local classifiers.

Bayesian Model Comparison `Bayesian_Model_Comparison`

Description: Bayesian model comparison, as implemented here, selects the best mixture of Gaussians model for the data. Each full candidate model is constructed using Expectation-Maximization. The program then computes the Occam factor and finally returns the model that maximizes the Occam factor.

Additional inputs: Maximum number of Gaussians for each models.

Component Classifiers with Discriminant Functions `Components_with_DF`

Description: This program uses logistic component classifiers and a softmax gating function to create a global classifier. The parameters of the components are learned using Newton descent, and the parameters of the gating system using gradient descent.

Additional inputs: The number of component classifiers.

Additional outputs: The errors through the training.

Component Classifiers without Discriminant Functions `Components_without_DF`

Description: This program works with any of the classifiers in the toolbox as components. The gating unit parameters are learned through gradient descent.

Additional inputs: A list of component classifiers and their parameters.

Additional outputs: The errors through the training.

ML_II `ML_II`

Description: This program finds the best multiple Gaussian model for the data, and uses this model to construct a decision surface. The program computes the Gaussian parameters for the data via the EM algoritm, assuming varying number of Gaussians. Then, the program computes the probability that the data was generated by these models and returns the most likely such model. The program then uses the parameters of this model to construct the Bayes decision region.

Additional inputs: Maximum number of Gaussians components per class.

Interactive Learning `Interactive_Learning`

Description: This program implements interactive learning in a particular type of classifer, specifically, the nearest-neighbor interpolation on the training data. The training points that have the highest ambiguity are referred to the user for labeling, and each such label is used for improving the classification.

Programs for Chapter 9

Additional inputs: The number of points presented as queries to the user, and the weight of each queried point relative the other data points.

Chapter 10

k-Means Clustering K_means

Description: This is a top-down clustering algorithm which attempts to find the c representative centers for the data. The initial means are selected from the training data itself.

Additional inputs: The number of desired output clusters, c.

Additional outputs: The number of the input patterns assigned to each cluster.

■ *k*-Means Clustering

<u>**begin initialize**</u> n, c, μ_1, μ_2, ..., μ_c

<u>**do**</u> classify n samples according to nearest μ_i

recompute μ_i

<u>**until**</u> no change in μ_i

<u>**return**</u> μ_1, μ_2, ..., μ_c

<u>**end**</u>

Fuzzy *k*-Means Clustering `fuzzy_k_means`

Description: This is a top-down clustering algorithm which attempts to find the k representative centers for the data. The initial means are selected from the training data itself. This algorithm uses a slightly different gradient search than the simple standard k-means algorithm, but generally yields the same final solution.

Additional inputs: The number of desired output clusters.

Additional outputs: The number of the input patterns assigned to each cluster.

◼ **Fuzzy *k*-Means Clustering**

begin initialize n, c, b, μ_1, μ_2, ..., μ_c, $\hat{P}(\omega_i|x_j)$, $i = 1, ..., c$; $j = 1, ..., n$

$\qquad\qquad$ normalize $\hat{P}(\omega_i|x_j)$

$\qquad\qquad$ **do** recompute μ_i

$\qquad\qquad\qquad$ recompute $\hat{P}(\omega_i|x_j)$

$\qquad\qquad$ **until** small change in μ_1 and $\hat{P}(\omega_i|x_j)$

$\qquad$ **return** μ_1, μ_2, ..., μ_c

end

Basic Iterative Minimum-Squared-Error Clustering `BIMSEC`

Description: This program iteratively searches for the c clusters that minimize the sum-squared error of the training data with respect to the nearest cluster center. The initial clusters are selected from the data itself.

Additional inputs: The number of desired clusters.

Programs for Chapter 10

■ Basic Iterative Minimum-Squared-Error Clustering

<u>**begin initialize**</u> $n, c, m_1, m_2,..., m_c$

    <u>**do**</u> randomly select a sample $\hat{x}$

        $i \leftarrow \arg min_i \|m_i - \hat{x}\|$ (classify $\hat{x}$)

        <u>**if**</u> $n_i \neq 1$ <u>**then**</u> compute

$$\rho_j = \begin{cases} \dfrac{n_j}{n_j + 1}\|\hat{x} - m_j\|^2 & j \neq i \\[2ex] \dfrac{n_j}{n_j - 1}\|\hat{x} - m_j\|^2 & j = i \end{cases}$$

        <u>**if**</u> $\rho_k < \rho_j$ for all j <u>**then**</u> transfer $\hat{x}$ to $\mathcal{D}_k$

        recompute J_e, m_i, m_k

    <u>**until**</u> no change in J_e in n attempts

<u>**return**</u> $m_1, m_{2}, ..., m_c$

<u>**end**</u>

Agglomerative Hierarchical Clustering AGHC

Description: This program implements the bottom-up clustering. The algorithm starts by assuming each training point is its own cluster and then iteratively merges the nearest such clusters (where proximity is computed by a distance function) until the desired number of clusters are formed.

Addition inputs: The number of desired clusters, c and the type of distance function to be used (min, max, avg, or mean).

■ Agglomerative Hierarchical Clustering

<u>**begin initialize**</u> $c, \hat{c} \leftarrow n, \mathcal{D}_i \leftarrow \{x_i\}, i = 1, ... n$

    <u>**do**</u> $\hat{c} \leftarrow \hat{c} - 1$

find nearest clusters, say, $\mathcal{D}_i$ and $\mathcal{D}_j$

merge $\mathcal{D}_i$ and $\mathcal{D}_j$

 until $c = \hat{c}$

 return c clusters

end

Stepwise Optimal Hierarchical Clustering SOHC

Description: This program implements the bottom-up clustering. The algorithm starts by assuming each training point is its own cluster and then iteratively merges the two clusters that change a clustering criterion the least, until the desired number of clusters c are formed.

Addition inputs: The number of desired clusters, c.

■ Stepwise Optimal Hierarchical Clustering

begin initialize c, $\hat{c} \leftarrow n$, $\mathcal{D}_i \leftarrow \{x_i\}$, $i = 1, \dots n$

 do $\hat{c} \leftarrow \hat{c} - 1$

 find clusters whose merger changes the criterion the least, say, $\mathcal{D}_i$ and $\mathcal{D}_j$

 merge $\mathcal{D}_i$ and $\mathcal{D}_j$

 until $c = \hat{c}$

 return c clusters

end

Programs for Chapter 10

Competitive Learning `Competitive_learning`

Description: This program implements competitive learning clustering, where the nearest cluster center is updated according to the position of a randomly selected training pattern.

Additional inputs: The number of clusters c, and the learning rate.

Additional outputs: The cluster index for each data point, and the weight matrix representing the cluster centers.

■ Competitive Learning

<u>**begin initialize**</u> $\eta, n, c, k, w_1, \dots, w_c$

$\qquad x_i \leftarrow \{1, x_i\}$, $i = 1, \dots, n$ (augment all patterns)

$\qquad x_i \leftarrow x_i / \|x_i\|$, $i = 1, \dots, n$ (normalize all patterns)

$\qquad j \leftarrow \arg max_j w_j^t x$ (classify x)

$\qquad w_j \leftarrow w_j + \eta x$ (weight update)

$\qquad w_j \leftarrow w_j / \|w_j\|$ (weight normalization)

$\qquad$ <u>**until**</u> no significant change in w in k attempts

$\qquad$ <u>**return**</u> $w_1, \dots, w_c$

<u>**end**</u>

Basic Leader-Follower Clustering `Leader_Follower`

Description: This program implements basic leader-follower clustering, which is similar to competitive learning but additionally generates a new cluster center whenever a new input pattern differs by more than a threshold distance θ from existing clusters.

Additional inputs: The minimum distance to connect across θ, and the rate of convergence.

Additional outputs: The number of the cluster assigned to each input pattern, and the final weight matrix.

Programs for Chapter 10

■ **Basic Leader-Follower Clustering**

<u>**begin initialize**</u> η, θ

$\qquad\qquad w_1 \leftarrow x$

$\qquad\qquad$ <u>**do**</u> accept new x

$\qquad\qquad\qquad j \leftarrow \arg max_j \| x - w_j \|$ $\qquad$ (find nearest cluster)

$\qquad\qquad\qquad\qquad$ <u>**if**</u> $\| x - w_j \| < \theta$

$\qquad\qquad\qquad\qquad\qquad\qquad$ <u>**then**</u> $w_j \leftarrow w_j + \eta x$

$\qquad\qquad\qquad\qquad\qquad\qquad$ <u>**else**</u> add new $w \leftarrow x$

$\qquad\qquad\qquad\qquad w \leftarrow w / \| w \|$ $\qquad$ (normalize weight)

$\qquad\qquad$ <u>**until**</u> no more patterns

$\qquad$ <u>**return**</u> w_1, w_2, ...

<u>**end**</u>

Hierarchical Dimensionality Reduction HDR

Description: This program clusters similar *features* so as to reduce the dimensionality of the data.

Additional inputs: The desired number of dimensions d' for representing the data.

■ **Hierarchical Dimensionality Reduction**

<u>**begin initialize**</u> d', $\mathcal{D}_i \leftarrow \{ x_i \}$, $i = 1, ..., d$

$\qquad\qquad \hat{d} \leftarrow d + 1$

$\qquad\qquad$ <u>**do**</u> $\hat{d} \leftarrow \hat{d} - 1$

Programs for Chapter 10

$$\text{computer } \mathbf{R}$$

find most correlated distinct clusters, say $\mathcal{D}_i$ and $\mathcal{D}_j$

$$\mathcal{D}_i \leftarrow \mathcal{D}_i \cup \mathcal{D}_j \quad \text{(merge)}$$

delete $\mathcal{D}_j$

until $\hat{d} = d'$

return d' clusters

end

Independent Component Analysis ICA

Description: Independent component analysis is a method for blind separation of signals. This method assumes there are N independent sources, linearly mixed to generate M signals, $M{\geq}N$. The goal of this method is to find the mixing matrix that will make it possible to recover the source signals. The mixing matrix does not generate orthogonal sources (as in PCA), rather the sources are found so that they are as independent as possible. The program works in two stages. First, the data is standardized, i.e., whitened and scaled to the range *[-1, 1]*. The data is then rotated to find the correct mixing matrix; this rotation is performed via a nonlinear activation function. Possible functions are, for example, odd powers of the input and hyperbolic tangents.

Additional inputs: The output dimension and convergence rate.

Additional outputs: The mixing matrix and the means of the inputs.

Online Single-Pass Clustering ADDC

Description: An on-line (single-pass) clustering algorithm which accepts a single sample at each step, updates the cluster centers and generates new centers as needed. The algorithm is efficient in that it generates the cluster centers with a single pass of the data.

Additional inputs: The number of desired clusters.

Basic Iterative Mean-Square-Error Clustering BIMSEC

Description: This program seeks the minimum of a global mean-squared-error criterion by iteratively adjusting cluster centers.

Additional inputs: The number of clusters, and the number of attempts to change the error.

Additional outputs: The cluster index for each data point and the error through the training.

Discriminant-Sensitive Learning Vector Quantization DSLVQ

Description: This program performs learning vector quantization (i.e., represents a data set by a small number of cluster centers) using a distinction or classification criterion rather than a traditional sum-squared-error criterion.

Additional inputs: The number of clusters.

Additional outputs: The final weight vectors representing cluster centers.

Exhaustive Feature Selection Exhaustive_Feature_Selection

Description: This program searches for the combination of features that yields the best classification accuracy on a data set. The search is exhaustive in subsets of features, and each subset is tested using 5-fold cross-validation on a given classifier.

Additional inputs: The output dimension, the classifier type, and the parameters appropriate to the chosen classifier.

Additional outputs: The indexes of the selected features.

Programs for Chapter 10

Information-Based Feature Selection `Information_based_selection`

Description: This program selects the best features for classification based on information-theoretic methods; the algorithm can be applied to virtually any basic classifier. However this program is often slow because the cross-entropy between *each* pair of features must be computed. Moreover, the program may be inaccurate if the number of data points is small.

Additional inputs: The desired number of ouput dimensions.

Additional outputs: The indexes of the features returned.

Kohonen Self-Organizing Feature Map `Kohonen_SOFM`

Description: This program generates a self-organized feature map or "topologically correct map."

Additional inputs: The dimensionality of the output space and the window width.

Multidimensional Scaling `MDS`

Description: This program represents a data set in a lower dimensional space such that if two patterns x_1 and x_2 are close in the original space, then their images y_1 and y_2 in the final space are also close. Conversely, if two patterns x_1 and x_3 are far apart in the initial space, then their images y_1 and y_3 in the final space are also far apart. The algorithm seeks an optimum of a global criterion function chosen by the user.

Additional inputs: The criterion function J_{ee}, J_{ef}, or J_{ff} (ee - emphasize errors, ef - emphasize large products of errors and fractional errors, or ff - emphasize large fractional errors), the number of output dimensions and the convergence rate.

Programs for Chapter 10

Minimum Spanning Tree Clustering `min_spanning_tree`

Description: This program builds a minimum spanning tree for a data set based on either nearest neighbors or inconsistent edges.

Additional inputs: The linkage determination method (`NN` - nearest neighbor, `inc` - inconsistant edge), and the number of output data points per cluster or difference factor.

Principle Component Analysis `PCA`

Description: This program implements principle component analysis. First the algorithm subtracts the sample mean from each data point. Then the program computes the eigenvectors of the covariance matrix of the data and selects the largest eigenvalues and associated eigenvectors. The data is then transformed to a new hyperspace by multiplying them with these eigenvectors.

Additional inputs: The desired output dimension.

Additional outputs: The reshaping matrix, the mean of the data and the matrix of eigenvectors used in reducing the dimension.

Nonlinear Principle Component Analysis `NLPCA`

Description: The program implements a neural network with three hidden layers: a central layer of linear units and two nonlinear sigmoidal hidden layers. The number of units in the central linear layer is set equal to the desired output dimension. The network is trained as an auto-associator—i.e., mapping input to the same target input—and the nonlinear principle components are represented at the central linear layer.

Additional inputs: The number of desired output dimensions, the number of hidden units in the nonlinear hidden layers.

Programs for Chapter 10

Linear Vector Quantization 1 LVQ1

Description: This program finds a representative cluster centers for labeled data, and can thus be used as a clustering or as a classification method. The program moves cluster centers toward patterns that are in the same class as the centers, and moves other centers away from those patterns of other classes.

Additional inputs: The number of output data points.

Linear Vector Quantization 3 LVQ3

Description: This program finds a representative cluster centers for labeled data, and can thus be used as a clustering or as a classification method. The program moves cluster centers toward patterns that are in the same class as the centers, and moves other centers away from those patterns of other classes. LVQ3 differs from LVQ1 in details of the rate of the weight updates.

Additional inputs: The number of output data points.

Sequential Feature Selection Sequential_Feature_Selection

Description: This algorithm sequentially selects features for the lowest classification error. Then, until enough features are found, a feature that gives the largest reduction in classification error is added to the set. For backward selection, the process begins with the full set of features, and one is removed at each iteration.

Additional inputs: The choice of search (Forward or Backward), the desired output dimension, the classifier type and associated classifier parameters.

Additional outputs: The indexes of the selected features.

Programs for Chapter 10

Genetic Culling of Features `Genetic_Culling`

Description: This program performs feature selection using a genetic algorithm of the culling type, i.e., it selects subsets. The algorithm randomly partitions the features into groups of size N_g. Each candidate partition is evaluated for classification accuracy using five-fold cross validation. Then, the algorithm deletes a fraction of the worst-performing groups and generate the same number of groups by sampling from the remaining groups. The whole process then iterates until a criterion classification performance has been achieved or there is negligable improvement.

Additional inputs: The fraction of groups discarded at each iteration, the number of features in each solution, the type of classifier and its associated parameters.

Additional outputs: The indexes of the final selected features.

References

1 R. O. Duda, P. E. Hart and D. G. Stork, **Pattern Classification** (2nd ed.), Wiley (2001)

2 The MathWorks, Inc., **MATLAB: The Language of Technical Computing**, The MathWorks, Inc. (2003)

3 I. D. Guedalia, M. London and M. Werman, "An on-line agglomerative clustering method for nonstationary data," *Neural Computation*, **11**:521-40 (1999).

4 K. Rose, "Deterministic annealing for clustering, compression, classification, regression, and related optimization problems, " *Proceedings of the IEEE*, **86**(1):2210-39 (1998)

5 M. Pregenzer, D. Flotzinger and G. Pfurtscheler, "Distinction sensitive learning vector quantization: A new noise-insensitive classification method," *Proceedings of the 4th International Conference on Artificial Neural Networks*, Cambridge UK (1995)

6 J. Friedman, "Regularized discriminant analysis," *Journal of the American Statistical Association*, **84**:165-75 (1989)

7 R. Meir, R. El-Yaniv and S. Ben-David, "Localized boosting," *Proceedings of the 13th Annual Conference on Computational Learning Theory*

8 E. Yom-Tov and G. F. Inbar, "Selection of relevant features for classification of movements from single movement-related potentials using a genetic algorithm," *23rd Annual International Conference of the IEEE Engineering in Medicine and Biology Society* (2001).

9 D. Koller and M. Sahami, "Toward optimal feature selection," *Proceedings of the 13th International Conference on Machine Learning*, pp. 284-92 (1996)

10 K.-R. Müller, S. Mika, G. Rätsch, K. Tsuda and B. Schölkopf, "An introduction to kernel-based learning algorithms," *IEEE Transaction on Neural Networks*, **12**(2): 181-201 (2001)

Index